POLICING ILLEGAL DRUG MARKETS:

Geographic Approaches to Crime Reduction

by

George F. Rengert

Jerry H. Ratcliffe

and

Sanjoy Chakravorty

Criminal Justice Press
Monsey, New York
2005

Dedication

To Kris and Justin and our West Philly days.
   – George Rengert

To Philippa.
   – Jerry Ratcliffe

To Shourjo, my son.
   – Sanjoy Chakravorty

363.45
R412p
2005

Cover design by Jerry H. Ratcliffe.

CONTENTS

LIST OF FIGURES AND TABLES

ACKNOWLEDGMENTS

The research reported in Chapters 5 and 6 was conducted under grant # 1999-IJ-CX-K005 from the U.S. National Institute of Justice. Points of view and opinions expressed in this book are those of the authors, and neither reflect nor represent the official policies or positions of the National Institute of Justice or the U.S. Government. We wish to thank Kristin Henderson and Tom Bole for assistance with the research contained in these chapters.

Parts of Chapter 4 were reprinted with permission of Criminal Justice Press from: George F. Rengert, Sanjoy Chakravorty, Tom Bole and Kristen Henderson (2000). "A Geographic Analysis of Illegal Drug Markets," in Mangai Natarajan and Mike Hough (eds.), *Illegal Drug Markets: From Research to Prevention Policy*, (Crime Prevention Studies vol. 11), Monsey, New York, Criminal Justice Press.

We owe a debt of gratitude to Jack O'Connell and the Delaware State Statistical Unit for the data used in this research. We would also like to thank Deputy Commissioners Patricia Giorgio-Fox and Charles Brennan, Suzanne Siegel and Rachel Weeden of the Philadelphia Police Department for additional data. Several people read and commented on previous drafts of this book. We would like to thank Eric McCord for his insightful comments on this book. And we wish to thank especially Marcus Felson, Jim LeBeau and Philippa Ratcliffe for their input into this project.

ABOUT THE AUTHORS

George F. Rengert is a professor of criminal justice at Temple University in Philadelphia, Pennsylvania. He holds an M.A. from Ohio State University and a doctorate from the University of North Carolina. A geographer by training, he is one of the founders of the modern field of spatial analysis in criminology. His area of specialty is the spatial and temporal behavior of property criminals. He is currently working on the application of geographic information systems to urban crime control. His previous books include: *Suburban Burglary: A Tale of Two Suburbs* (Charles C Thomas); *The Geography of Illegal Drugs* (Westview Press); *Suburban Burglary: A Time and a Place for Everything* (Charles C Thomas); *Metropolitan Crime Patterns* (Willow Tree Press); *Crime Spillover* (Sage); and *Campus Security: Situational Crime Prevention in High-Density Environments* (Criminal Justice Press).

Jerry H. Ratcliffe is an associate professor of criminal justice at Temple University. A former police officer with the Metropolitan Police in London (UK), he has conducted research in the areas of environmental criminology and police intelligence practice in the U.S., Australia and the U.K. His books include *Strategic Thinking in Criminal Intelligence* (Federation Press) and *GIS and Crime Mapping* (John Wiley).

Sanjoy Chakravorty, chair of the Department of Geography and Urban Studies at Temple University, is primarily interested in issues of development and distribution as they relate to spatial and social change. His papers have been widely published in geography, development, economics, planning, and urban and regional journals, and his research has been funded by the National Science Foundation, the U.S. National Institute of Justice, the American Institute of Indian Studies, and the World Bank. His forthcoming publications include two books: *Fragments of Inequality* (Routledge) and *Made in India* (Oxford). More information on Dr. Chakravorty's work (including some current papers) may be found at http://astro.temple.edu/sanjoy.

1. INTRODUCTION

This book analyzes the social, economic, and environmental conditions that attract street-level drug dealers to specific locations within our cities. It also focuses on the response of public officials to these conditions. This is not an insignificant undertaking. The sale of illegal drugs is a massive problem for public officials in the U.S. Billions of dollars are spent annually addressing this problem in our nation. For many years at the national level, about two-thirds of this effort has been directed at the enforcement of illegal drug laws rather than the treatment of addicts (Reuter and MacCoun, 1992). The enforcement effort has met with varying success, especially when measured in terms of permanent sustained results. The problem addressed in this book is why sustained results have not accompanied this massive effort.

Some critics argue that government officials would not need to spend billions of dollars confronting illegal drugs if we would simply legalize currently illegal drugs (Nadelmann, 1988). These resources could then be focused on other problems facing our society. This point of view states that the problem is one we have simply created for ourselves. In chapter 2, we address this issue and explain why illegal drugs are an important public policy issue associated with harms that public officials are justified in addressing.

A large proportion of the illegal drugs consumed in America is derived from agricultural crops grown in foreign countries. The policy of the United States government is to discourage foreign countries from growing the crops that our illegal drugs are derived from (Office of National Drug Control Policy, 1997; Reuter, 1992). The drug problem in the United States would be much less severe if crops from which illegal drugs are produced were not grown in foreign countries. On the other hand, the producing nations point out that they would not have problems associated with the illegal production of a drug if the demand did not exist in the United States. Chawla (2004:90) illustrates how this debate often is framed at the United Nations:

Country A has a large problem with the consumption of a particular drug – cocaine or heroin. Country B produces a lot of that cocaine or heroin. Country A says to Country B, "Stop your production and supply, because my poor people are getting addicted and dying." Country B says to Country A, "Stop your consumption, because your demand is pulling and sustaining my supply." The result is a deadlock because it is not easy to establish the extent to which a market is supply or demand-driven.

This issue is addressed in the second chapter of this book.

In the third chapter, the traditional roles of the police in the effort to control the supply and demand for illegal drugs in the United States are identified and evaluated. These efforts include interdiction at the wholesale levels as well as demand reduction through educational efforts focused on the youth of our nation. Many of these police functions are extremely popular with the general public, although they have not been successful in controlling illegal drug sales and use. The third chapter contains a discussion of what has gone wrong with these programs and why they are not associated with sustained success measured in terms of reduced illegal drug use in our society.

Chapters 2 and 3 identify the reasons why our government policies – which are focused on supply regions, wholesale distribution into and throughout our nation, and local demand reduction efforts – have not experienced sustained results. Perhaps new methods and approaches that will be more successful in the future can be developed. The central theme of this book is to highlight one such approach that has not attracted sufficient attention. This is to identify why illegal drugs are sold at particular places. If we can identify why illegal drugs are sold at particular places, perhaps public policy can be developed to remove these advantages and incentives. The remainder of this book addresses this issue.

In Chapter 4, we deal directly with the economic reasons why illegal drugs are sold in some places rather than others. In this chapter, illegal drugs are conceptualized to be similar to any other product with a retail sales structure. Just as we can identify a best place to locate a grocery store or bank in a region, we can identify the best places to sell illegal drugs in a region. In Chapter 4, we test whether or not we can successfully predict where illegal drugs are sold using these economic principles. These are areas of the city that are most accessible to those who are potential customers for illegal drugs.

A limitation of this analysis is that relatively large areas are defined within which illegal drugs are sold. These areas are identified by measuring the straight line distances from drug markets to potential customers. In this case, the spatial nature of the local transportation infrastructure is not considered. Nor are the exact sites identified from which illegal drugs are likely to be sold within the relatively large areas. In the words of Lersch (2004), we have identified spaces rather than places from which illegal drugs are sold.

Chapters 5 and 6 introduce a relatively new method of predicting which particular places or sites will be chosen by illegal drug dealers. These are places central to local demand, anchors for routine activities of potential customers for illegal drugs, and, transportation nodes that funnel regional customers into and throughout the city. Using techniques recently introduced to the fields of criminal justice and criminology, sites of illegal drug sales are identified. Put another way, reasons why illegal drugs are sold at particular places and not at others are identified. These reasons are conceptualized as problems that public officials can address. (A detailed discussion of the modeling framework used in the study is presented in the Technical Appendix.)

Chapter 7 places the police squarely in the center of this process by arguing that they are the public officials best able to identify problems associated with particular sites from which illegal drugs are sold. This approach is termed problem-oriented policing (Goldstein, 1979). This chapter also addresses why facilities traditionally identified as a problem for a local neighborhood in fact may not be the major contributing factor to a place being a site for illegal drug sales.

Chapter 8 sets out the tasks for police in problem-oriented policing. Especially important is identifying the public agencies that, in cooperation with the police, may address these problems. The police alone cannot solve all the problems associated with illegal drug sales. They can steer other public agencies in the correct directions to assist in this effort. Many examples of this cooperative effort are identified in this chapter.

The approach identified in this book may not be the easiest approach or the one that is most satisfying to the general public. Yet it may be the approach that is most likely to be associated with sustained results. The final chapter contains the argument for problem oriented policing focused on places where illegal drugs are sold as a partial solution to our nation's illegal drug problem.

Our hope is that we as a nation move beyond the easy solutions that are politically popular because they focus the blame for illegal drugs on others, to solutions we address as a group, taking responsibility on our own shoulders. It is a well known axiom that blaming keeps us helpless since it requires changes over which we do not have direct control. Problem-oriented policing involves taking responsibility for changes and shepherding them through public and private agencies. In this book, we identify the various forms of blaming used by our political officials and set them to rest so that effective approaches may be identified. But first, we must address the argument that there would not be an illegal drug problem if our country would simply legalize all currently illegal drugs. We must confront the argument that illegal drug use is a victimless crime that only harms those who choose to use illegal drugs. In other words, why should the American public be concerned with illegal drug use?

2. WHY WE SHOULD BE CONCERNED ABOUT ILLEGAL DRUGS

Illegal drugs are a great concern to the government and citizens of the United States. One reason for this concern centers on the many costs society bears surrounding drug addicts. There are various estimates of how much drug users cost the rest of us. Alan Leslie (1971) computed that the typical heroin addicts on the streets of New York City in 1970 cost tax payers an average of $14,000 per year. Mehay (1973) used this figure to estimate the total social cost for the country to be between $4 and $8 billion dollars a year. Rengert (1996) updated these figures to argue that in modern times, with current prison and policing costs and more reasonable crime costs, the figure is more like $135,427 per addict per year. And this is not as high as Zedlewski's (1989) estimate of $430,000 per year for crimes committed by an average released convict. Clearly, the public has a right to be concerned.

Table 2-1 provides an estimate of how many people in our country are chronic and occasional illegal drug users. These figures illustrate that, in general, there are fewer heroin and cocaine users now than in the past decade. On the other hand, methamphetamine and marijuana use is on the increase. Illegal drug users number in the millions. The health and welfare costs for those who choose to use illegal drugs, are also significant. For example, in a single year (1997) Florida reported that nearly 40,000 hospitalizations were linked to drug abuse, increasing hospital costs by $304 million. This did not include more than $350 million for treating diseases and other health disorders caused by substance abuse, $46 million for detoxifying substance-addicted patients, and about $8 million for the delivery and care of newborns affected by maternal substance abuse and addiction (Florida, 1999). Newborn babies are especially troubling since they have no choice in the matter of becoming drug addicted.

Table 2-1. Estimated Number of Chronic and Occasional Drug Users (in thousands), 1988-2000

Drug	1988	1989	1990	1991	1992	1993	1994	1995	1996	1997	1998	1999	2000
Cocaine (occasional)	6,000	5,000	4,600	4,478	3,503	3,332	2,930	3,082	3,425	3,487	3,216	3,216	3,035
Cocaine (chronic)	3,984	3,824	3,558	3,379	3,269	3,081	3,032	2,866	2,828	2,847	2,800	2,755	2,707
Heroin (occasional)	170	150	140	359	304	230	291	428	455	597	253	253	253
Heroin (chronic)	1,341	1,266	1,119	1,015	955	945	932	923	910	904	901	898	898
Meth-amphetamine (chronic)	274	269	259	270	302	381	474	584	664	707	669	617	595
Marijuana (total)	11,600	10,900	10,200	10,400	9,700	9,600	10,100	9,800	10,100	11,100	11,000	11,900	12,100

Source: Drug Availability Steering Committee (2002), *Drug Availability Estimates in the United States* (Washington, DC: Drug Enforcement Administration).

Another idea of the nature and scope of the health and welfare problem can be obtained by examining Drug Abuse Warning Network (DAWN) data for just one illegal drug – heroin. Although not comprehensive, DAWN data give an idea of the severity of the health-related substance abuse problems in our nation. DAWN data are collected from participating hospital emergency rooms and medical examiners. For emergency rooms, DAWN reports the number of patients seen for drug-related problems. This information is supplemented by data from participating Medical Examiners' Offices where deaths are listed as drug-induced and drug-related deaths. These data are gathered from 35 sites in 21 metropolitan areas in the United States. Table 2-2 lists this data. This data shows that 4,832 deaths were heroin-related in the sample of medical examiners and 62,511 heroin-related patients were seen in this sample of emergency rooms in the year 2000. For the entire United States, the figures would be much higher. Furthermore, if we add the health-related incidents for the other illegal drugs, one obtains a picture of the magnitude of the health-related issues surrounding illegal drug use in the United States.

Many of these illegal drugs are grown and produced in foreign countries and smuggled into the United States for final distribution. Given the volume of drugs smuggled into the United States, this is not a simple task. The Drug Availability Steering Committee (2002) estimates that about 350 pure metric tons of cocaine, 125 pure metric tons of methamphetamine, and 15 pure metric tons of heroin were smuggled into the United States in 2001. When one speaks of tons, one is speaking of considerable volume. This is a massive undertaking. In response, the United States expends money and personnel in attempting to secure our borders and prevent the influx of illegal drugs. Judging by the drug-related impact on the medical system (Table 2-2), this expenditure would not appear to be totally successful.

Not all drugs are imported. A majority of marijuana plants (Pulse Check, 2002; Rengert, 1996; Trebach, 1987) and a large proportion of methamphetamine supplies (Drug Availability Steering Committee, 2002) are produced within our borders. Controlling these drugs is clearly within our jurisdiction. More controversial is our attempt to control the source of illegal drugs that are not produced within our borders. This effort is referred to as "source control" (Rengert, 1996).

Incomplete knowledge of basic principles of geographic analysis can lead to ineffective foreign policy in this instance. For example,

Table 2-2. Drug Abuse Warning Network Data: 2000

(showing a comparison of heroin-related Medical Examiner-recorded deaths [ME] and Emergency Room [ER] visits)

City	ME	ER
Atlanta	30	485
Baltimore	397	5,405
Birmingham	3	
Boston	183	3,867
Buffalo	30	
Chicago	499	12,454
Cleveland	48	
Dallas	94	478
Denver	66	666
Detroit	296	3,328
Kansas City	20	
Las Vegas	93	
Long Island, NY	105	
Los Angles	473	3,177
Louisville	10	
Miami	86	1,452
Milwaukee	4	
Minneapolis/St Paul	17	
New Orleans	57	982
New York	607	11,009
Newark	179	4,399
Norfolk, VA	24	
Oklahoma City	19	
Omaha	2	
Philadelphia	461	4,661
Phoenix	181	841
Portland, OR	107	
St. Louis	55	1,084
Salt Lake City	80	
San Antonio	90	
San Diego	145	1,031
San Francisco	148	2,756
Seattle	118	2,490
Washington, DC	84	1,946
Wilmington, DE	21	
Total	4,832	62,511

Source: Drug Availability Steering Committee (2002), *Drug Availability Estimates in the United States* (Washington, DC: Drug Enforcement Administration), table 2-17, page 71.

before expending millions of dollars on source control, officials developing these tactics should have obtained data on how many regions of the world have environmental conditions conducive to growing an illegal drug. Also, the relative influence of the United States government in these various regions requires consideration. Clearly, if we are successful in disrupting the flow of illegal drugs in the short run, supply and demand principles suggest that the value of the commodity will increase and there will be an incentive for other entrepreneurs in other parts of the world to begin production. For example, the United States government was successful in lowering the acreage devoted to the opium poppy in Turkey. But the U.S. has not been successful in controlling the increased production in Iran, Pakistan, Mexico and Myanmar (formerly known as Burma), which negated this success in Turkey. Even Colombia is entering this lucrative market, and undercutting the price from Southeast Asia. Ginsberg (2002:13) describes this competitive process:

> With the cocaine craze slipping (but still strong) in the United States, the cartels diversified. They imported Asian poppies, planting significant acreage; engineered a snortable, more powerful powder; slashed the price; and started sending heroin north. Columbians figured they could skirt the fear of needles and HIV and trump the pricier product from Asia. . . . It was a pure market grab. By the late 1990s, Colombian heroin has usurped the place of Afghan and Burmese heroin on the U.S. East Coast and was making inroads nationwide.

Heroin is not the only illegal drug the United States government has tried to control in a foreign country without long-term success. The same scenario has occurred with cocaine. The United States Government has been successful in lowering illegal production of the coca plant in Bolivia and Peru. But it has been unsuccessful in countering increased production in Columbia and Venezuela. Basic principles of geographic diffusion, and economic principles of supply and demand, should have shown policy makers that millions of dollars spent on source control are not likely to be successful when measured in terms of the long-term supply reaching the borders of the United States.

The point of this discussion is to illustrate that illegal drug use is a serious problem within this country, a problem that we are not likely to solve in someone else's country. We must focus our attention within our borders, over which we have jurisdiction. The problem of reducing the flow of illegal drugs into and within our country is massive. Simply note the amount of illegal drugs crossing our borders every year. Although we are not certain of the exact amounts (since drug smugglers do not share these figures with academic researchers), we are getting better at estimating what these figures are (though the accuracy of these figures varies by type of drug). Experts agree that we are more accurate in estimating the amount of cocaine imported into the United States than other illegal drugs such as heroin or methamphetamine (Drug Availability Steering Committee, 2002). Table 2-3 gives these estimates in ranges for various illegal drugs in pure metric tons. It also illustrates how many metric tons of these drugs have been seized by federal officials. If we subtract these two columns, we have an estimate of the pure metric tons of each illegal drug that reaches our cities, comes under the jurisdiction of local law enforcement, and is marketed by entrepreneurs in these localities (these figures do not include locally produced methamphetamine and marijuana).

Consider again the argument that the United States would not have many of these problems if it simply would legalize all currently illegal drugs (Nadelmann, 1988, 1992). The main argument against legalization of illegal drugs is that it would exacerbate health and welfare problems (Goode, 2005; Inciardi and McBride, 1989). For example, Sweden experimented with a program of legal prescriptions in the 1960s. It was a short-lived experiment because, in the wake of the program, drug use rapidly increased (Knutsson, 2000). This increased drug use is related to health and welfare expenses that the citizens of the country must bear.

Since the 1960s, the arguments for legalization, or at least decriminalization, have become more coherent (Mieczkowski, 1992). Proponents of decriminalization of some drugs argue that the consequences

Table 2-3. Drug Availability Estimates (in pure metric tons)

Drug	Amount Imported	Federal Seizures	Street Availability
Cocaine	366-376	106	260-270
Heroin	15.5-20.5	2.5	13-18
Methamphetamine	113.6-143.6	3.6	110-140
Marijuana	11,215-25,215	1,215	10,000-24,000

Figures derived from Drug Availability Steering Committee (2002), *Drug Availability Estimates in the United States.* (Washington, DC: Drug Enforcement Administration).

of the "war on drugs" have included frequent violations of suspects' rights, exaggeration of the dangers of drugs (an exaggeration that runs counter to the experiences of many youths), and the ignoring of the profits of drug selling that motivate lower-class youths into the realm of drug dealing and crime (Kaplan, 1983; Kraska, 1990). There is also the opportunity to refocus law enforcement toward those drugs that remain criminalized, as well as a reduction in expenses across the whole criminal justice system. Opponents of decriminalization cite the risk of increased drug use, as well as a risk of increased crime, a moral decline and the confusion of a government message that appears to accept drug use (Kraska, 1990). As Kraska goes on to note however, the arguments for decriminalization are "with a few exceptions, vague, unrefined, and disparate. If decriminalization arguments are to have any effect, they must be clearly stated with specific recommendations for policy" (1990:132). Given that the unwavering tone of the government argument for the last half century has been that drugs are evil, it is likely that a U-turn in policy would be close to political suicide. A thorough treatment of the legalization/decriminalization dispute is beyond the scope of this book, but Goode (2005) provides an overview of this debate.

Arguments for and against legalization or decriminalization aside, the reality is that certain drugs are illegal in the United States, and this situation is unlikely to change in the immediate future. Discussions of drug legalization are essentially moot in the present political climate. In fact, we may see tobacco use criminalized before we find marijuana legalized. Note that more and more areas are being designated as "smoke free."

It should be recognized that illegal drugs have an adverse impact not only on the health and welfare of the drug user, but also on communities in which they are sold. Since they are illegal, drug dealers and customers do not have access to the criminal or civil justice systems to solve disputes. In these instances, they must resort to violence in order to "tighten up business" and/or resolve disputes. Customers may resort to property crime to obtain funds to support their habit or dependency. Rengert (1996) illustrates how these drug-dependent property crimes tend to cluster spatially around illegal drug market places. Clearly, urban communities, illegal drug users, and the American public that pays criminal justice, crime, health, and welfare costs, are all adversely affected by illegal drug use.

The focus of this book is on local drug markets. It is the authors' opinion that source-control efforts are doomed to failure and probably are unethical. They are doomed to failure because the United States has limited influence over many drug-producing regions of the world. It is unethical to expect another country to change its laws and policies to solve our problems, especially countries where a specific drug is not illegal. For example, the coca leaf is brewed into a tea served in hotels in Peru and is commonly chewed by farmers working in the fields (Rengert, 1996). A certain number of hectares are licensed by the national government to farmers to legally produce this crop. Should they stop the production of cocaine because the United States has a problem with cocaine and crack consumption? Consider how United States' citizens would react if Peruvians asked us to stop growing tobacco because Peruvian citizens die from the effects of United States-produced tobacco (deaths that are actually occurring). Many of the countries that are net exporters of illegal narcotics are laboring under severe international debts, and are vulnerable to U.S. pressure. This pressure forces them to expend personnel and resources on crop control and supply reduction, a cost for tackling (usually unsuccessfully) a problem that is not necessarily a significant local priority. In many cases, they would probably prefer to spend that money on other areas of the economy that would produce a long-term, local benefit (e.g., health care or education). However, the grants and loans that they receive from the U.S. often come with conditions that extort a hefty price, requiring the money to be spent as the donor sees fit rather than by local need.

As a country, we should concentrate our efforts within our own borders rather than blaming others and attempting to solve our nation's problems in someone else's country. We have an unfortunate history of blaming and focusing our efforts outward (as exemplified by the slogan "war on drugs," implying an outside enemy on which force is used). In this book, we will focus on the lowest level of illegal drug distribution – retail sales, the final destination of the journey of illegal drugs. The impact of local efforts may be greater than efforts focused on higher levels (Reuter and Kleiman, 1986). For example, our borders are so extensive that they will never be completely sealed (Reuter, 1990). Wholesale distribution is very clandestine, with sales restricted largely to known and trusted customers. It is at the local level that sales become more open, more detectable, and more preventable. Local enforcement not only affects local supply, but as illustrated by Knutsson (2000:191), it also affects local demand:

> When the police start targeting street markets . . . there will initially be an increase in the number of detected offenders and reported crimes. However, the market is likely to adapt to the increasing risks, dealing will be done more discreetly, and in less public sites. . . . This means that it will be harder for the police to detect crimes, and, more to the point, the availability of drugs will decrease for those who do not have any connections with the drug scene . . . (t)he most vulnerable groups are youths, who will be exposed to a situation with more limited access to drugs.

Knutsson (2000) illustrated that this scenario happened exactly in Sweden. He divided Swedish drug enforcement history into three periods: (1) a time when police did not put much effort on street markets; (2) a time when police started targeting street markets; and, (3) a time when the police had been targeting street markets for about a decade. In the first period, those under age 25 accounted for about 55% of all drug crimes. During the second period, there was a marked increase in absolute numbers but a decrease in the proportion of those under 25 years of age, who accounted for less than 40%. In the final period, those under 25 declined both in absolute numbers and percent to about 20% of drug offenses. The decline was especially notable for those 15 to 17 years of age. Clearly, when we make it difficult to obtain drugs, the impact is felt most strongly among the youngest potential drug users.

There is a tendency for those unfamiliar with drug use to assume that all drug users are alike (and different from you and me!). Many believe that once you start taking drugs, you will become physiologically addicted and will do whatever is necessary to obtain illegal drugs. Becker (1953), however, demonstrated that many illegal drug users are dabblers who are not physiologically addicted. Other potential drug users have yet to experiment with illegal drugs. When we make illegal drugs less available through street-level enforcement, we reduce the number of illegal drug users in our society, as illustrated by Knuttson (2000) in Sweden. Street-level drug markets are the focus of this book. The authors are especially concerned with how distributors choose a retail sales location and the impact of this decision on the local community. But first we must consider the efforts of the federal government to control the supply of illegal drugs. Both successful and unsuccessful efforts in our country and abroad are examined.

3. POLICE RESPONSES TO ILLEGAL DRUGS

In the previous chapter we highlighted a number of reasons why illegal drugs are a concern to the general population. The number of drug users, the societal cost of each drug addict, as well as the number of drug-related emergency room visits across the country are all a cause for concern for individual citizens and society in general. These concerns would be more tolerable if there was any indication that interdiction efforts were having an effect on the domestic drug market.

Reuter (1990) noted that increased interdiction should theoretically increase the price of drugs. However, the increased law enforcement effort in the last few decades appears to have had the reverse effect. Prices have been steadily falling (Caulkins, 1998; Reuter, 1997). Reuter's conjecture is that increased enforcement has had a number of effects that are detrimental to the effectiveness of border enforcement. For example, greater law enforcement inadvertently has resulted in the development of a corps of experienced and expert smugglers who have been able to remove the inexperienced competition. Furthermore, greater interdiction has actually increased production in source countries because, if the demand stays the same but more drugs are intercepted, greater production is required to maintain the same supply level. This seems almost counterintuitive, but if thought through, it makes sense. An increase in detections and confiscations, without successfully reducing demand, merely encourages drug producers to increase production to supply the ever-present demand and negates the value of interdiction. Finally, greater interdiction may have forced drug importers to diversify into smaller, more effective transport mechanisms that are harder to detect. In essence, we have forced drug importers to adapt and become so proficient that our detection methods are relatively ineffective.

Seizures at the American border are not the only inconveniences facing illegal drug importers. Law enforcement officials in both source and transit countries can hamper the international illicit drug trade. For example, opium traffic through Afghanistan's southern border had tailed off in 2001 due to a ban on production imposed by the Taliban regime. In fact, the Taliban, with this one edict, was probably more successful in stemming the flow of drugs than the Western democracies had been in the previous two decades (UNODC, 2003).

The overthrow of the Taliban regime by the United States and U.S.-backed forces unfortunately paved the way for a rapid increase in opium poppy cultivation back to pre-edict levels. While this U.S. operation might have temporarily upset the operational plan of some terrorist groups, it certainly seems to have put Afghanistan's drug traders back into business.

As a measure of the scale of the drug trade in this region, consider the case of Iran. Located on the southern border of Afghanistan, Iran is considered to be at the front line in the war on heroin. Drug seizures in Iran are both significant in size, and occasionally violent. Table 3-1 lists only a few of the drug seizures in Iran, but it is clear that the proximity to Afghanistan creates an opportunity for drug interdictions of significant quantities. Accurate figures of interdiction efforts are difficult to establish, but if Iranian law enforcement intercepts up to half the drugs passing through their country, then the scale of the drug business in this volatile part of the world is huge, and the remaining

Table 3-1. Examples of Drug Seizures in Iran, July 2000

PLACE OF SEIZURE	DATE	DRUG TYPE	QUANTITY (KG)	METHOD OF TRANSPORTA-TION	METHOD OF SEIZURE
Mianch	July 11th	Morphine	1,000	vehicle	checkpoint
Taibad	July 16th	Hashish	20	camel	gun battle
Kerman	July 22nd	Morphine	710	backpack	gun battle
Bam	July 23rd	Opium	298	truck	checkpoint
Torbat-e-Jam	July 25th	Opium	163	backpack	gun battle

Source: Islamic Republic of Iran's Anti-Drugs Newsletter, July 2000. Note that morphine is a derivative of opium, and like opium is the basic ingredient in heroin.

undetected drugs constitute a significant problem for destination countries.

All this suggests that law enforcement internationally, as well as on the national borders of the United States, is affecting drug interdiction on a large scale, albeit with varying success. The value of interdiction efforts overseas and on United States borders can only be ascertained by the impact on the domestic drug markets.

Figures 3-1 and 3-2 show that street-level drug prices for cocaine and heroin decreased almost continually from 1981 to 2000, while at the same time the street-level purity increased for heroin. Although street-level purity for cocaine decreased slightly throughout the 1990s, levels still remain high and the street price is dropping. Most source

Figure 3-1. Average U.S. Retail Price and Purity for Cocaine Purchases of One Gram or Less

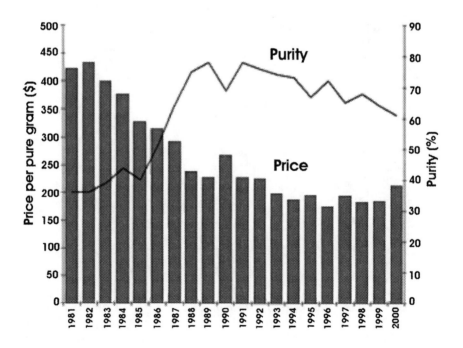

Source: Office of National Drug Control Policy, "National Drug Control Strategy Update 2003," February 2003.

Figure 3-2. Average U.S. Retail Price and Purity for Heroin Purchases of 0.1 Gram or Less

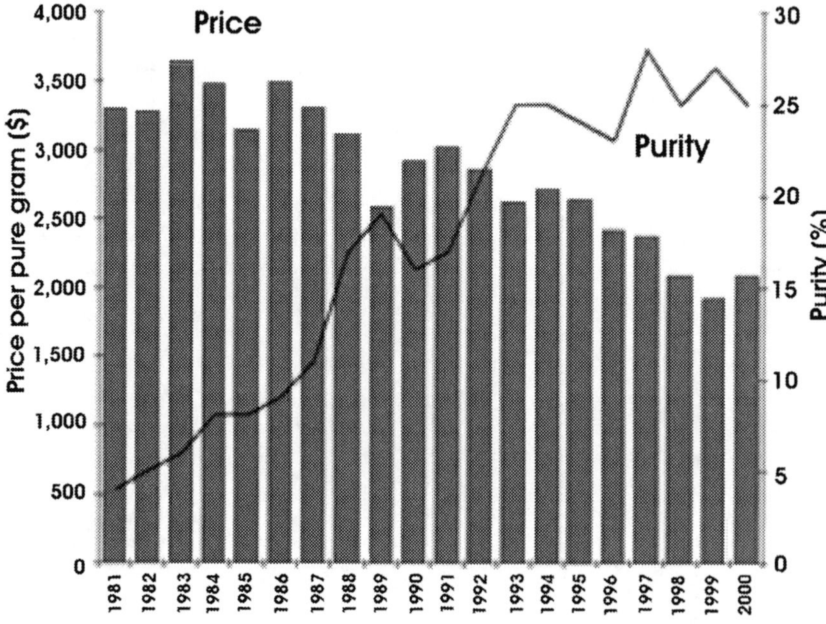

Source: Office of National Drug Control Policy, "National Drug Control Strategy Update 2003," February 2003.

countries are producing illicit drugs at only a fraction of their capacity (Rengert, 1996). Therefore, illicit drugs lost through interdiction can be easily and cheaply replaced by the source country.

Caulkins and Reuter (1998) have estimated the cost components for cocaine sold at retail in 1990 in the United States (Table 3-2). These figures suggest that the price of producing and importing cocaine is only about 13% of the street price. If we remove production costs, Caulkins and Reuter (1998) estimate that seizures of all forms by all levels of government account for only about 8 to 11% of the retail price of cocaine. Producing countries can replace cocaine seizures at a cost of about 1% of street value. The costs of drug production and avoiding seizure prior to reaching the United States are therefore less than one-

Table 3-2. Components of the Street Price of Cocaine

Wholesale Price in Colombia	1%
Importing of Drug	12%
Retail Labor	13%
High-level Labor	~3%
Drug and Asset Seizures	8-11%
Money Laundering Fees	2-4%
Packaging, Processing and Inventory Costs	~2%
Compensation for Risk of Prison	23%
Compensation for Physical Risk	33%

quarter of the street price of the drug, hardly indicative that these are significant threats or hindrances to the international drug business.

Price and purity figures indicate that interdiction efforts have not been successful in changing the domestic drug trade in any meaningful way. If interdiction had been more successful, we might expect to see an increase in the price of illegal drugs driven by lack of drug availability, or a decrease in purity based on the need to cut a limited drug supply to make it go further among the drug user community. As neither an increase in price nor a significant decrease in purity is apparent, we conclude that although the best efforts of the international and federal law enforcement community are providing a modest barrier to illicit drugs entering the country, that barrier is a very porous one.

It is a reality that drugs can flow easily into the United States. However, as Reuter (2000) has pointed out, drugs are a commodity and have to be sold. Selling requires a marketplace. If policing at organizational levels above local law enforcement are unable to stem the amount of drugs entering our country over the long run, the question remains, what can local law enforcement do to limit retail drug markets? In the following discussion, traditional methods practiced by local police are discussed.

CHARACTERISTICS OF LOCAL DRUG MARKETS

We must realize that all retail illegal drug markets are not alike. There have been many attempts to categorize them into types (Eck, 1994;

Rengert, 1996; Reuter and MacCoun, 1992). For present purposes, we will simplify these into a dichotomy.

Later in this book, different types of local drug markets are examined. For the following discussion, two broad types are considered:

(1)   an outdoor market with regional customers; and,

(2)   an indoor market with a network of largely local customers.

Outdoor markets conduct business on the street. If they are conducting transactions with regional customers who travel into the area, then, like fast food restaurants, the best locations for these markets are near thoroughfares and transportation interchanges. In contrast, if business is conducted inside a dealer's home, then the customers are most likely part of a network that is linked to the dealer either by personal contact with someone who knows the dealer or because the customers live in the dealer's neighborhood.

It is also worth noting that drug markets of either type are dynamic and responsive to external and internal factors. For example, if a local community of users is uprooted to other locations when rehousing takes place (such as the demolition of a high-rise public housing project), a static drug market at the old location would rapidly lose business. It therefore is possible that the dealers may either choose to move with their customers to a new location, or to diversify into a market focused more toward a regional customer base.

Outdoor markets seem particularly sensitive to enforcement action and appear able to adapt. By moving indoors and relying on a network of customers, the dealers often are able to conduct business beyond the eyes of street-level law enforcement officers, who require a warrant to search indoor premises. By removing the market from public space, dealers are reducing the ability of law enforcement to act against them.

This adaptability to the effects of law enforcement can be seen in Figure 3-3, where the proportion of tips that related to indoor or outdoor drug activity fluctuated considerably over a two-year period. During this period, the Philadelphia Police exerted considerable effort on Operation Safe Streets, a project that aimed to place a police officer on every one of over 300 drug-dealing street corners (outdoor sales) in the city. Throughout 2002 it can be seen that the proportion of calls to the anonymous city tips line that related to outdoor drug sales activity fell in comparison to calls in regard to indoor drug markets. The increase during the summer of 2003 was probably due to either an improvement

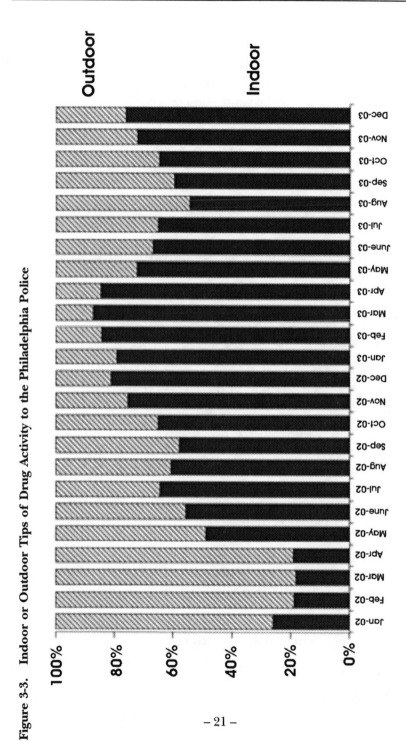

Figure 3-3. Indoor or Outdoor Tips of Drug Activity to the Philadelphia Police

in the weather, making street drug activity more comfortable for all parties, or a decrease in the efficiency of the Safe Streets operation, possibly from what Sherman (1990:10) calls *crackdown decay*, where there is a "bureaucratic regression to the mean level of effort." In other words, it is possible that initial police enthusiasm for the Safe Streets program waned, or that officers became bored or disillusioned with permanent posting to a single street corner. There are a variety of possible explanations for the pattern seen in Figure 3-3; however, the point is that adaptation and evolution of drug markets would appear to be a perpetual process that is responsive to factors such as law enforcement activity.

The two types of drug markets identified above are dynamic and adaptable, and while enforcement action may be successful in the short term, it also may cause an adaptation to a market of another type and/or in another location in the long term. As noted in the previous chapter, this adaptation may make drugs less available to the uninitiated potential drug user – a good outcome. On the other hand, what other tactics are available to the police to impact this less accessible mode of illegal drug distribution? One option that is popular is to address demand for illegal drugs directly, as with the DARE program.

Drug Awareness Resistance Education (DARE)

Probably the most recognized attempt at reduction in long-term drug use in the United States is the DARE program. It was developed in 1983 through a collaboration of the Los Angeles Police Department and the Los Angeles Unified School District. With little evaluation of its effectiveness, it grew rapidly and continues to be a huge law enforcement/community collaboration effort. By 1996, DARE had reached into 70% of the nation's school districts, with about 25,000 police officers trained to teach the 17 core classes (Sherman et al., 1998). DARE is the most frequently used substance abuse education program in the United States. To many in America, DARE is synonymous with antidrug education. It is advertised with bumper stickers on cars and shirts with the DARE logo worn by both children and adults. As noted by Carter (1995:7): "In philosophy and practice, DARE complements the tenets of a community based approach to policing."

Recent evaluations raise serious questions about the long-term value of DARE. The DARE web site does list one study that "proves" that DARE works, a study by Dr. Joseph Donnermeyer of Ohio State

University. The web page where this reference is cited tells visitors to the site: "Looking for research or evaluations on the DARE program? Searching for links for additional resources? Explore no more" (DARE, 2004). It would appear that the DARE staff does not want to encourage us to look any further than this one study! Unfortunately, the study in question does not appear to actually address the issue of reduced drug use among children, but simply asks teachers and parents if they think the DARE training is effective. Thinking that a program is effectual is not the same as it actually being effective. The full report is not generally available to the public.

Those less inclined to take DARE America's word for it, and who make the effort to search a little further, may find an altogether different story. In a review of published and peer-reviewed studies of DARE, a research team funded by the U.S. National Institute of Justice concluded that while there were some minimal short-term effects in places, there was no overall impact of DARE on long term drug use patterns (Sherman et al., 1998). As evidence, the authors cited a number of multi-year longitudinal studies, which concluded that the short-term effects wore off quickly and that after a period of time there was no difference in the tendencies to use drugs between groups that had, and had not, undergone DARE classes (Clayton et al., 1996; Rosenbaum et al., 1994; Sigler and Talley, 1995). One study actually concluded that drug use among kids in the suburbs had increased for the group that underwent DARE education (Rosenbaum and Hanson, 1998). In this case, the research team concluded that, "Policy makers, searching for a magic bullet to the drug problem, have expected too much from a single program. Compounding the problem, parents, educators, and police officers have confused program popularity with program effectiveness" (Rosenbaum and Hanson, 1998:381).

This gets to the core of the problem with many well-meaning programs. We like to think that they work, but if the core aim is a long-term reduction in drug use among children or adults, then there is a need to be realistic (sometimes brutally so) about program effectiveness. We should heed the words of Charles Darwin in his famous debate with a clergyman concerning evolution of species: "I have not yet acquired that command over my understanding that would allow me to believe what I want without evidence." It seems that too many framers of public policy feel they have gained that level of command. If DARE, the largest nationwide attempt to reduce the demand for illicit drugs among children is unsuccessful, then police efforts may be better focused on the supply or marketing of drugs in our communities rather than on demand reduction. This is not to say that we should discontinue our efforts at demand reduction through advertisements in the public media and drug treatment programs. Rather, the police may not be the best source of such programs. DARE programs that rely on "scared straight" tactics have not been any more successful than other programs that rely on this concept (Sherman et al., 1998). Police efforts may best be focused on enforcement and problem identification associated with drug sales places. Again, this effort is best conducted with the cooperation of the community the police serve.

DARE program administrators have tried to respond to the empirical criticisms. However, changes in response to criticism have not been evaluated and their success is not known. DARE meanwhile continues to have widespread support and the cost of the program continues. And this illustrates a common problem with attempts at long-term crime reduction: image is often more important than substance. Police do not have to actually reduce crime in the long term, they simply have to be seen to be doing something in the short term. They often use tactics that do not have any long-term benefit. DARE is a central component of community policing, and in terms of image-management (style over substance), it has been argued that community policing is simply another tactic in a long line of image-management policing strategies (Barlow and Barlow, 1999).

COMMUNITY POLICING

Observers of policing contend that we are in a community policing era (Walker and Katz, 2001). The late 1980s saw a move toward a more meaningful relationship with the community that the police serve. Concerning illegal drugs, Moore and Kleiman (1997:231) highlight the importance of a police-community relationship:

> Police strategists must consider that the assets available to attack the drug problem are not limited to the money and legal powers channeled through the police department. The community itself has resources to deploy against drug trafficking and use. Indeed, without the community's own efforts at self-defense, it is hard to see how the police can possibly succeed.

Community policing has its origins in the lack of police interaction with the community that led to the "crisis of legitimacy" of the police during the time of the urban race riots in the 1960s (Sherman et al., 1998). Too heavily focused on efficient law enforcement, rapid response and the rule of law, the police were urged to increase the level and quality of community contact. This was deemed especially important if the police were to combat illegal drug sales.

Within policing there was a recognition that public support was required in the fight against illegal drug sales. Advocates of community policing recognized that the existing model of policing was unable to be responsive to community concerns, and that police have a central role in the community that allows them potentially to engage local organizations not directly associated with law enforcement in the war on crime. External to the police, there was a move to return responsibility for crime control back to the community. The rise of suburban sprawl had reduced community cohesion in many areas of our cities as community leaders left the city. This led to a decrease of community support for the local police. The regaining of this support is a driving force behind the move toward community policing. The police were increasingly being told to be more accountable to the community. This need for increased contact with the community was perceived to be a problem not only in the United States, but also in the United Kingdom (Tilley, 2003), suggesting a wider movement for reform in policing.

In the decades that have followed, community policing has come to be broadly defined as: "A collaboration between the police and the community that identifies and solves community problems" (CPC, 1994:1). Community policing has come to mean increased engagement with the community by the police, not at a superficial level, but through a restructuring of the police organization and a change in the priorities of the workload of operational officers. While there will always be a need for some response policing, the aim of community policing is to have officers engaging with local residents and helping them solve the concerns of local people. In other words, to remove the conditions of crime before the crime occurs. In the case of drug sales, this would involve removing the conditions conducive to an illicit drug market before a market is established. This thought will be central to the analysis and conclusions that follow.

Cordner (1995) identified four dimensions to community policing: philosophical, tactical, organizational and strategic. First, all officers must be aware of and subscribe to the central tenets of the community policing philosophy, which place the community at the center of police prioritization. At the street (tactical) level, the police organization should instigate community-oriented programs such as block organizations and mini-police stations, while also educating officers in problem-solving approaches to community problems. At the organizational level, the police must move to a more decentralized method of operation that empowers officers to identify problems and solve them at the street level. Finally, there should be a strategic move toward a greater emphasis on crime prevention in comparison to offender apprehension. This stage requires a revision of the ways that a police organization rewards officers and recognizes success.

Among the difficulties with community policing is the definition of the "community." While a community can often find a consensus as to what the local problems are, the "community" can actually be a small group who are vocal and able to influence police and may not represent the broader community (Bohm et al., 2000). Second, the police role changes significantly with community policing, and this requires some retraining of officers. But the available evaluations have found that this often does not take place (Breci, 1997). In other instances, police resist carrying out community policing functions (Uchida et al., 1992). Finally, community policing is seen as "soft" by some officers, who have grown accustomed to the crime-fighting image that they envisage for themselves (Sadd and Grime, 1995b; Walker and Katz, 2001).

Some of the initiatives that are implemented in the name of community policing do not work. The best example, though one that is still implemented in various places with depressing regularity, is Neighborhood Watch (NW). Neighborhood Watch is a police-community partnership in which local citizens either (at the more conservative end of the implementation) hold meetings and work with their neighbors to keep an eye on things, or (at the more extreme end) patrol the streets and sidewalks of their neighborhood. NW members report any suspicious activity to the local police, who then take formal action if the incident is verified as criminal. In effect, the Neighborhood Watch participants are the eyes and ears of the local police. As an example,

Figure 3-4. Society Hill Town Watch

community activists patrol the Society Hill area of Philadelphia, a neighborhood with roots going back to the signing of the Declaration of Independence at the local Independence Hall (see Figure 3-4).

However, as Sherman and his colleagues point out, this type of program has been evaluated on numerous occasions with the same overall result – Neighborhood Watch does not reduce crime (Sherman et al., 1998). In fact, in some cases it can have the negative effect of increasing the fear of crime (Skogan, 1990).

The evidence about community policing as a response to drug markets is mixed, mainly because some of the solutions that are termed "community policing" fall better under the mantle of problem-oriented policing (see next section). Where there is strong community involvement in issues of drug markets, reviews are not generally positive. For example, while concluding that there had been some benefit to Chicagoans from community policing, Skogan and Hartnett (1997) recount an example where local police and a local church minister worked together to organize two anti-drug marches to street corners where an outdoor drug market was believed to be operating. Unfortunately, local enthusiasm waned and the second march was not well attended by a broad cross-section of the community.

Similarly, an early community effort in 1985 in Philadelphia saw the formation of United Neighbors Against Drugs (UNAD) in the Norris Square area of the city. The group highlighted the local drug program with rallies and initial efforts looked promising. Although there was police cooperation, there was little long-term impact. The organization dissolved quickly after two UNAD leaders were assaulted by drug dealers and a police captain who had worked closely with the group was transferred. In March 1998, a coalition of nine neighborhood organizations reformed UNAD to tackle not only drugs but also larger community concerns. The anti-drug focus waned quickly, however, as a local police commander was again reassigned (Weingart et al., 1994). Now renamed the Norris Square Neighborhood Project, the group's work is more focused on community improvement (www.nsnp.org).

In the late 1990s, the U.S. Bureau of Justice Assistance (BJA) funded a demonstration program called the "Innovative Neighborhood Oriented Policing" (INOP program). INOP was designed to support the development of community policing strategies and tactics at the neighborhood level with the goal of reducing the demand for drugs through community involvement and interagency cooperation (Sadd and Grime, 1995a). In each of the eight cities studied, evaluators concluded that implementation problems plagued the projects. There were three main areas of concern. First, the officers assigned to community policing duties continued to encounter problems overcoming patrol officer resistance to the principles of community policing. The program was seen as soft and for lazy officers, and recruitment of officers to the community policing program was difficult. Secondly, INOP sites had problems generating interagency support for community policing and struggled to get other agencies involved. Where contacts were made, they were personal contacts that were lost when the officers were reassigned. In the end, the administrative aspect of the community seemed to not be highly involved in "community" policing. Finally, the INOP sites had difficulty in generating active community involvement, with officers describing the community as apathetic. This most intractable of problems is summarized by the evaluators (Sadd and Grime, 1995b):

> Even the most knowledgeable community leaders in most of the sites, however, had only a limited understanding of the goals of the projects or, most importantly, their role in community policing. Many community leaders were baffled by the idea of "partnerships" and could not explain what they were expected to do in these partnerships. The most common response to the question, "What do the police mean when they ask for the community's help?" was that the police expected residents to call them with information regarding criminal activities. However, this is what the police have always asked the public to do.

In summary, although there are examples of some successes with what is locally defined as community policing, it is difficult to contend that community policing can be an effective tactic against drug markets when the words mean different things to different people (Correia, 2000). Furthermore, there is significant evidence that community policing is not an effective tactic in creating long-term crime reduction. The authors of a significant survey of the long-term effectiveness of crime prevention initiatives note that community policing without a clear focus on crime-risk factors generally shows no effect on crime (Sherman et al., 1998). Perhaps the police and the community need a clearer focus than is implied in a general term such as community policing. There is more to addressing illegal drug markets than simply getting to know the neighbors and neighborhood cooperation with the police. It is difficult to sustain enthusiasm for marches and demonstrations over the long run. In contrast, changes in the physical environment and environmental design may have longer-term effects. Such a focus is provided in problem-oriented policing.

Problem-oriented Policing

From its beginnings in the 1980s with Herman Goldstein's work with the police department in Madison, Wisconsin, the problem-oriented policing model has been adopted by many police agencies in the United States, the United Kingdom, Canada, Scandinavian countries, Australia, and New Zealand (Center for Problem-Oriented Policing, 2004). A real boost to problem-oriented policing came with the funding of the federal Violent Crime Control and Law Enforcement Act of 1994, which created the Office of Community Oriented Policing Services (COPS) to support projects that had a community policing element. What is interesting is that the COPS office definition of community policing is " . . . a policing philosophy that promotes and supports organizational strategies to address the causes and reduce the fear of crime and social disorder through problem-solving tactics and police-community partnerships" (COPS, 2004:1). While problem solving is not a strict requirement for a COPS grant, it is clear that the inclusion of "problem-solving tactics" in the definition of the major funding body has helped to focus interest in problem-solving methods. This has helped both to develop problem-oriented policing as a legitimate policing style, and to link problem-oriented policing and community policing in the minds of many members of the public and the police.

Problem-oriented policing has been described as: "An approach/method/process within the police agency in which formal criminal justice theory, research methods, and comprehensive data collection and analysis procedures are used in a systematic way to conduct in-depth examination of, develop informed responses to, and evaluate crime and disorder problems" (Boba, 2003:2). Where problem-oriented policing differs from community policing is that it places the spotlight on innovative crime-reduction strategies, whether these involve the local community or not. As Sherman and colleagues state: "Where the core concept of community policing was community involvement for its own sake, the core concept for problem-oriented policing was *results*: the effect of police activity on public safety, including (but not limited to) crime prevention" (Sherman et al., 1998:8-6, emphasis in original).

Problem-oriented policing requires a clear description of a focused problem. For example, "vehicle crime" is far too broad an issue for a problem-oriented policing strategy; however, vehicle thefts from a city center car park are a better defined and more manageable problem. The fact that this (hypothetical) car park is located next to a large inner-city high school further defines the problem. Finally, the fact that it is open on all sides with no physical barriers to those who wish to walk through the car park creates a clear picture of the problems associated with this car park. The emphasis with problem-oriented policing is on tailoring solutions to individual problems associated with individual crime sites or issues. The process begins with the clear definition of the problem in hand so that crime analysis can be used to describe the key features of the problem. Sometimes however, an accurate identification of the problem to be analyzed is the most difficult part of the process (Nicholl, 2004).

Problem-oriented policing has been successful in a number of drug-related case studies. Two case studies published by the COPS Office document local initiatives that were successful in very different environments. Police officers in Delray Beach, Florida were able to significantly reduce the instances of outdoor drug dealing around a local store by enacting solutions that had little to do with ideas of traditional law enforcement but managed to achieve a longer-term improvement in the local environment. Over time, the local officers instigated a nuisance-abatement suit against a local drug house, arranged for the installation of bullet-proof security lighting, arranged fire chief approval and blocked a local alley that was popular with drug dealers, repaired a local chain link fence, painted the store, installed a fake security camera and redesigned the parking area at the front of the store. The overall effect was a dramatic reduction in drug activity as well as a reduction in the number of calls for service to the area (Sampson and Scott, 1999).

In another example, the residents of a Brooklyn, New York neighborhood worked with police to create a collaborative committee that investigated building code violations and worked with the local criminal and civil justice systems to close down a building that was at the center of local drug activity. Building violations also were used as the reason to close down a corner restaurant that was used as a drug retail market in Portland, Oregon. The restaurant corner was also subject to police and community activity in redesigning the physical environment in order to discourage outdoor drug dealing (Sampson and Scott, 1999).

What is noticeable about these examples is the primary focus on outdoor drug markets. The examples are all of markets that are located in commercial areas or near commercial attractions in residential neighborhoods. While it is unclear from the examples, it would appear likely that the consumers are likely to be regional residents who visit the neighborhood specifically for the purposes of buying drugs. These markets also would be attractive to local youths who had yet to develop a network of suppliers, but must rely on the open advertising of street level drug dealers to attract their attention.

SUMMARY

In this chapter we have argued that focusing of our energies overseas is counter-productive to solving the drug problem in America. While some countries are making valiant attempts to inhibit the flow of drugs to the U.S., the sheer strength of the demand dwarfs any gains made in the war on drugs. There seems to be an ongoing political will to concentrate resources on enforcement. That being the case, we argue that these resources are best used at the local law enforcement level, and see problem-oriented policing as a promising tactic.

With a focus on having street officers take the initiative by identifying and solving problems, problem-oriented policing seems ideally suited to many of the retail drug markets that are such a problem in urban America. These problems may be rooted in the economic, social, and/or physical environments of our cities. The task is to identify the problems related to illicit drug sales that can be tackled by police, other public agencies, and the community. One objective is to take the profit out of illegal drug sales. This leads us to consider where in the city are the most profitable locations to sell illegal drugs. These places can be identified using methods developed in economic geography to determine where the best places to locate legitimate retail establishments are. In the following chapter, these methods are applied to determine which locations in Wilmington, Delaware are the most suited for illegal drug sales.

4. THE LOCATION OF ILLICIT DRUG MARKETS: AN EXAMINATION OF ECONOMIC PRINCIPLES

We know that drug markets tend to cluster spatially in socially disorganized inner-city neighborhoods (Olligschlaeger, 1997; Forsyth et al., 1992; Kleiman, 1991). However, we do not know whether the drug distributors initially sought out such neighborhoods (Eck, 1994), or whether they located in neighborhoods which had locational advantages from a marketing perspective and their drug sales led to the social disorganization of the neighborhoods (Rengert, 1996; Rengert and Wasilchick, 1990). In other words, is the problem the social disorganization of the neighborhoods that attracts drug sales or the location of the neighborhoods with respect to potential customers of illegal drugs? Also, it is not clear why drug dealers choose to establish markets in one neighborhood and not in another when both seem to have similar socio-economic and demographic characteristics. That is, the locational principles and agglomeration economies which make certain neighborhoods more desirable to drug dealers have not been identified in their entirety.

If problem-oriented policing is to have an impact, we first must identify the problems to be solved. In the following analyses, we address these issues and provide police and policy planners with the means to predict the outcomes of their activities. These outcomes include where illegal drug markets will diffuse if they are ignored, or be potentially spatially displaced if police concentrate their attention on a specific area in the city. We especially are interested in identifying those problems associated with illicit drug markets that can be addressed to alleviate the situation. Many of these problems have an economic and geographic basis to them. The following studies have been instrumental in identifying these drug-dealing areas.

The Drug Market Analysis Program

At the beginning of the last decade, the U.S. National Institute of Justice funded a series of studies titled the Drug Market Analysis Program (DMAP). These studies provided important findings concerning the geographic setting of illegal retail drug markets (Maltz, 1993). They focused on five cities: San Diego, Jersey City, Pittsburgh, Kansas City, and Hartford. Three of these sites produced important findings concerning the spatial characteristics of illegal retail drug markets.

Eck's (1994) analysis focused on San Diego. He determined that there was not just one type of illegal drug market. He suggested that illegal retail drug markets could be categorized into four types, using contrasting concerns for security on the part of drug dealers and their customers:

- Neighborhood;

- Open regional;

- Semi-open regional; and

- Closed regional markets.

This classification results from the interaction of two variables. The first is whether the customers are local or regional. The second is whether the location of the drug market attracts customers or whether customers determine the location of the drug market through a social network. The first variable is closely related to Reuter and McCoun's (1992) categorization of drug markets based on whether customers were residents of the transaction neighborhood, or whether they were generally outsiders who brought money into the neighborhoods where the drug transactions occurred. If the customers were largely outsiders, the markets tended to be open and located near major thoroughfares that funnel customers into the region. If the customers were local, markets would tend to be closed and to be located at sites most accessible to the local demand. Thus, locations catering to nonresidents can be very different from those serving a local clientele.

Weisburd and Green (1995) studied drug markets in Jersey City, New Jersey. They determined that illegal drug markets were spatially concentrated. They mapped "intersection areas" that were hot spots of illegal drug sales, and discovered that these drug hot spots made up only 4.4% of the street intersections of Jersey City. However, these "hot spots" accounted for approximately 46% of narcotics sales arrests. These results illustrate the degree to which illegal drug markets were spatially concentrated in Jersey City.

Previous research proposed the theoretical reasons why drug markets are expected to concentrate in space. Kleiman (1991:9-10) argued: "Drug transactions are highly concentrated geographically, almost certainly more concentrated than consumption, with a strong bias toward poor and socially disadvantaged neighborhoods. . . . Sellers cluster for the same reasons fish shoal and birds flock: protection from natural enemies, in this case the police. Since police routines tend to create a distribution of officers which is more uniform than the distribution of illicit activity, being the sole dealer on a corner is far riskier than being one of twenty. Buyers, too, insofar as they face enforcement risk, face much less of it in a crowd than they would alone."

Rengert (1996) suggests a second explanation for the geographic concentration of drug dealers: illegal retail drug sellers tend to concentrate in space due to "agglomeration economies." Much like the sales locations of automobiles, once an area becomes known as a source region, buyers will travel to this location to obtain illegal drugs. The more dealers there are at a specific location, the more likely it will be that drugs of choice are available, and the more buyers will patronize this location. There are therefore at least two theoretical reasons to expect retail drug dealers to concentrate in space. Weisburd and Green (1995) found such concentration in Jersey City, New Jersey.

Olligschlaeger (1997) studied illegal drug sales in Pittsburgh. His analysis moves beyond describing where illegal drug markets are located by attempting to predict where they will be sited in the future. He developed a spatio-temporal forecasting method (chaotic cellular forecasting, based on neural networks) for use as an early warning system for police and public policy analysts concerned with the location of emerging illegal drug markets. He was successful in tracking displacement in time and space, and in identifying new hot spots before street patrol officers were aware of their existence. He also found that the illegal drug markets were concentrated geographically.

These studies used various types of police data to identify drug markets. In San Diego, Eck (1994) used police records of arrests, calls for service, and patrol information. He also collected information from agencies other than the police on the type of building structure where the dealing occurred. In Jersey City, Weisburd and Green (1995) used police arrest data for drug offenses and for crimes assumed to co-vary with the location of illegal drug markets. In Pittsburgh, Olligschlaeger (1997) supplemented police data on drug-related calls for service and arrests with data from the revenue office on property ownership, tax evaluation, and property characteristics.

Two important geographic principles concerning the retail sales of illegal drugs emerged from these studies: (1) illegal drug markets tend to be spatially concentrated; and (2) the location and characteristics of these markets will vary depending on whether the customers are local or regional. These are two fundamental components of the drug problem at the local level, and essential considerations for law enforcement if an effective solution is to be formulated. While we have suggested that problem-oriented policing shows great potential in alleviating local drug problems, the technique is not without its difficulties, one of which has been the quality of the problem analysis (Eck, 2004). We suggest that, at a minimum, police wishing to apply a problem-oriented policing solution must be able to establish the spatial extent of the drug problem, and the size and nature of the customer base.

The research we present below will build on these principles to determine whether the locations of illegal drug markets in Wilmington, Delaware can be predicted using variables that measure the relative size of the local demand.

Characteristics of Wilmington, Delaware

Wilmington is an excellent environmental laboratory in which to examine illegal drug sales. It is a small city that is also part of a large agglomeration (the Philadelphia metropolitan area), and that manifests many of the features considered typical of older East Coast cities in the United States. Wilmington is a central city for the state of Delaware, with large proportions of minority and lower middle class populations living in largely segregated conditions. High-rise buildings dominate the downtown (see Figure 4-1).

Wilmington is well served with a regional and local transportation infrastructure. A major interstate highway (I-95) bisects the city, and the Amtrak commuter rail system has a stop within Wilmington. Other major highways funnel traffic into the city, so Wilmington maintains a well-developed transportation infrastructure. A breakdown of popula-

Figure 4-1. Wilmington, Delaware Viewed from the South

tion statistics from the 1990 Census (the period central to this study) follows:

population: 71,516

white: 42%

black: 52%

other: 6%.

In the Census data, males tended to be younger than females, with the average age of women in Wilmington at 38.3 years, while the average age of men was 33.4. Nearly one-third of the people in Wilmington over the age of 24 did not graduate from high school (32.3%). In 1990, 17.6% of the population was deemed below the poverty line. The average household income was $35,064. Of the just over 31,000 housing units in the city, 8.6% were vacant and about one-third were rental properties.

Wilmington contains a surprisingly wide variety of environments for a city of its size. Housing types range from the very expensive in the northwest to the very modest in the center and southeast (see Figure 4-2). The city has an active port, as well as numerous financial institutions and corporate headquarters. Finally, it contains a small tourist and entertainment industry.

There are a variety of locations that theoretically should attract illegal drug dealers in Wilmington. In the following analyses, we determine whether or not we can identify locations of illegal drug sales arrests using a combination of economic principles of marketing and theoretical explanations taken from the criminology literature. The models are described in the following sections. We are focusing on drug sales arrests at the exclusion of arrests for drug possession since police often follow a purchaser a few blocks before making an arrest. Arrests for drug sales are more likely to take place at the location of the sales activity. Also, as pointed out by Kleiman (1991), drug possession is less concentrated spatially than drug sales.

THEORETICAL BACKGROUND

Given what we know about the social and demographic characteristics of drug users and sellers, the history of neighborhood viability in the face of drug dealing, and the geographic clustering of crimes around drug trafficking locations, it seems reasonable to expect the following scenario to unfold. Initially, a local entrepreneur chooses a site from which to sell drugs (possibly his or her home). When a spatially fixed site is first chosen for drug sales, the dealer must choose a location where the nearest residents are disorganized enough to not know, not care, or feel helpless to confront the drug dealer. This scenario generally involves a crack or heroin distributor located in a deteriorating neighborhood along a street dominated by rental housing, industry, or an uncontrolled local park. If the neighborhood is not disorganized, resistance to the drug dealer can become violent (Zucchino, 1993; Lacayo, 1989; Goodman, 1990). If effective neighborhood resistance is not forthcoming, the drug dealer may establish a fixed-site distribution location. However, this site will persist only if it has locational advantages so that enough customers find it to be a relatively attractive place to purchase

Figure 4-2. An Affluent Neighborhood in Wilmington

illegal drugs to remain profitable (Rengert et al., 2000; Rengert and Rengert, 1989).

Hough and Edmunds (1997) apply two useful concepts from marketing geography to illustrate the relationship between a market area and the profitability of a drug-dealing site. These concepts are threshold population and range. The threshold population is the number of customers necessary to make a profit. The range is the distance that customers are prepared to travel to purchase a commodity from a specific site. A market will be stable, or will grow, if the population threshold – the minimum number of people needed to sustain it – lies within the market's range. Figure 4-3, adopted from Hough and Edmunds (1997), illustrates how threshold and range can interact to yield thriving and failing markets. Rengert (1996) used these concepts to categorize illegal drug-market places.

The Mechanisms of Neighborhood Breakdown

Two counteracting forces are evident in illegal drug markets. In order to remain profitable, a stable or growing population of customers must be located within the range of the site. On the other hand, the spatial clustering of crime around drug markets (Rengert, 1996; Weisburd and Green, 1995) is likely to drive local residents from their homes. The scenario is likely to be as follows; as more and more users become dependent on a source of drugs and continue to seek the means to support their addiction, crime is expected to expand greatly in the vicinity of the drug market places. A significant proportion of this crime is expected to focus spatially on the neighborhoods immediately surrounding the drug market. Stable community residents in the neighborhoods surrounding a fixed-site distributor will sense the threat to the stability of their local area (Kennedy, 1993). Many will personally experience a residential burglary or street crime (Lacayo, 1989). They may decide to stay and fight back with increased community organization, block watches, and increased demands for police services (Rasmussen et al., 1993). They also may "harden" their properties with alarms, bars on windows, and increased security at entry points of previous burglaries (Rengert, 1996), as demonstrated by the business in Figure 4-4.

However, many of the family-oriented residents are likely to become dissatisfied with the community because of the deterioration in the

Figure 4-3. Threshold and Range in an Illegal Drug Market

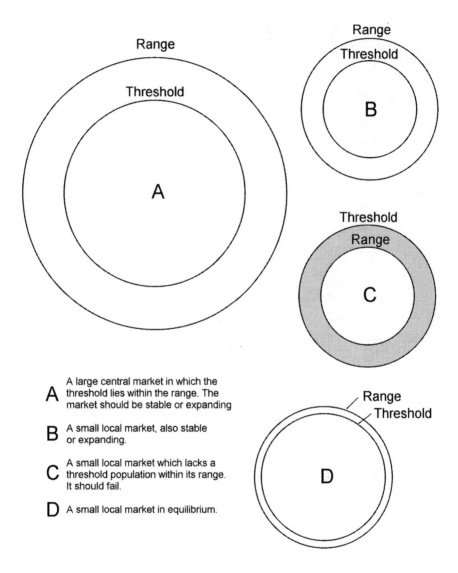

A A large central market in which the threshold lies within the range. The market should be stable or expanding

B A small local market, also stable or expanding.

C A small local market which lacks a threshold population within its range. It should fail.

D A small local market in equilibrium.

Figure 4-4.   A Storefront Completely Enclosed in Bars

quality of the neighborhood for family living, and then to seek a safer environment within which to live (Morganthau, 1989). Those who are financially able may move to a less crime-ridden neighborhood. This leaves some abandoned homes as residents leave faster than they are able to sell their homes (Lacayo, 1989). Prospective homeowners and renters are reluctant to purchase or rent homes in high-crime and drug-infested neighborhoods (Taylor, 1995). Financial institutions hesitate to loan money to new buyers in these neighborhoods for fear of losing their equity as home prices plummet. New homebuyers thus are forced to pay cash for homes in the community. Even home improvement loans to owners of rental property become hard to find. As the more stable members of the community move out, the remaining neighbors' ability to resist drug distributors and crime is reduced (Zucchino, 1993).

As the neighborhood's ability to resist the activities of drug distribu-tors and the associated property criminals decreases with the out-migration of stable community members, an opportunity is created for drug distributors to expand the spatial base of their activities. As the area becomes known as a source of illegal drugs, the profits from sales expand greatly. Fixed-site drug distributors may add additional sellers on neighboring blocks. Competing sellers also enter the market and may position themselves as close to other sellers as agglomeration economies allow (Rengert, 1989). More than one distributor now operates from the same neighborhood during most hours of the day. Most drug buyers come to the location on foot or by public transportation in the city (Pettiway, 1993). Crime focuses on this neighborhood to such an extent that, over time, it tends to become a persistent high-crime area (Schuerman and Kobrin, 1986). Many dealers commence selling from the street corners rather than from inside establishments. The range of sales expands markedly if the location is well sited because buyers no longer need to be familiar with the neighborhood (or the local habits of the supplier – where he will be and when) to purchase drugs.

If most of the homeowners have now abandoned this neighborhood, residential burglary as well as other drug-dependent property crime focuses on the zone surrounding this exhausted "fished out" area. This surrounding area also begins to lose community residents who can afford, and want, to leave. This leads to community disorganization in a new area, which reduces these neighbors' ability to resist the establishment of competing drug sellers who expand into their neighborhoods. In other words, in the absence of concentrated police attention, illegal drug sales and drug-related crime would begin to diffuse outward in a contagious fashion from the initial sales site. This is the general scenario believed to be associated with drug markets (Rengert, 1996). Carried to its logical extremes, whole regions of the city would be devastated, such as the South Bronx in New York City or the "Bad Lands" of Philadelphia.

What the above scenario ignores are basic geographic concepts associated with marketing illegal drugs. If most of the residents leave a neighborhood, a market will lose threshold conditions required to remain in business. The only tradeoff is if the dealers expand the range of the market. In order for this to occur, the location must be accessible to customers arriving other than by foot. In other words, the location must be accessible to automobile and/or public transportation routes. By the latter stages of the scenario outlined above, street dealing becomes commonplace. With street dealing, buyers require less specific knowledge of individual dealing locations in an area, and therefore private car use increases on the part of the buyers, who can simply cruise a known drug area seeking street-corner dealers.

Not all neighborhoods are so located. These locations must be within easy driving distance of major thoroughfares, or within quick walking distance of transportation nodes like train or subway stations and bus stops (Block, 1995). For instance, Eck (1994) discovered that in San Diego outdoor drug markets formed at locations within about two blocks of major transportation arteries. Block and Davis (1996) and Loukaitou-Sideris et al. (2002) found that crime tended to cluster around transit stations. Loukaitou-Sideris (1999), Levine and Wachs (1986), and Levine et al. (1986) discovered that crime clustered in and around bus stops. These locations would be required if local demand declined with neighborhood deterioration. Therefore, neighborhoods not located near transportation nodes require local demand to remain in business. However, local demand may be insufficient if local residents abandon the area.

Setting aside the issue of regional customers for the moment, the question is whether or not an illegal drug market can remain stable if it depends solely on local customers. There is a difference of opinion in the literature on this issue. For example, Boyum (1992) argues that retail dealers are essentially never driven out of business by negative accounting profits since so many of the costs involved are risk compensation. On the other hand, Reuter and Kleiman (1986), Hough and Edmunds (1997) and Rengert (1996) argue that retail markets can be put out of business by lowering their profits. In the following analysis, we will disentangle this issue.

The Location-Allocation Model of Illegal Drug Sales

There are a variety of locations that theoretically should attract illegal drug dealers. We used police arrest data for illegal drug sales to identify spatial concentrations of illegal drug sales in Wilmington. However, one problem with police arrest data is that police may stop making arrests while an illegal market is still operating. This policy is called "containment" (Rengert, 1996; Schuerman and Kobrin, 1986), and it occurs when police write-off an area while concentrating on keeping the sale of drugs from spreading to surrounding communities. To check that this was not occurring in Wilmington, we tested for the temporal consistency of the spatial arrangement of illegal drug-sales arrests. Figure 4-5 illustrates that there was temporal consistency in drug sales arrests across census tracts, with no evidence of any areas where drug sales arrests were high one year and the police stopped making arrests in the following years.

We used data from the years 1989, 1990, and 1991 (at the census tract level) so as to be close to the 1990 census data used later in this analysis. The census tract is an enumeration unit that on average contains about 4,000 people. The problems inherent at this aggregation – over-inclusiveness and error-prone border effects – are well known. Yet, the census tract is the most widely used intra-urban analytical unit in the U.S.

Figure 4-6 illustrates the spatial arrangement of drug sale arrests in Wilmington as a kernel density surface. This figure also demonstrates the spatial concentration of drug sales arrests in a few census tracts located in central and eastern Wilmington.

In the following analysis, we determine whether we can identify the high ranked census tracts using models of retail marketing developed in geography. We focus on the demand of local addicts. If an illegal drug dealer wishes to serve the needs of local addicts, that dealer would first need to identify their individual characteristics. In marketing geography, we use demographic profiling to determine the characteristics of a hypothetical person who would have the greatest demand for illegal drugs.

Demographic Profile of Demand for Illegal Drugs

There have been many studies that identify the characteristics of addicts. These studies generally agree with the findings of the National Household Survey on Drug Abuse (U.S. Department of Health and Human Services, 1993) that addicts tend to be young (15-29 years of age), to have attained less than a high school education, and to be unemployed in the formal economy. These variables formed the basis of our demographic profile of the local spatial demand for illegal drugs.

Other studies also have identified and used these variables in the analysis of illegal drug use. Olligschlaeger (1997) used a younger age profile of 12 to 24 years to identify the population at risk of drug use in Pittsburgh. However, in Inciardi's (1995) sample of heroin users, he found the median age of first use to be over 18 years. Only alcohol had

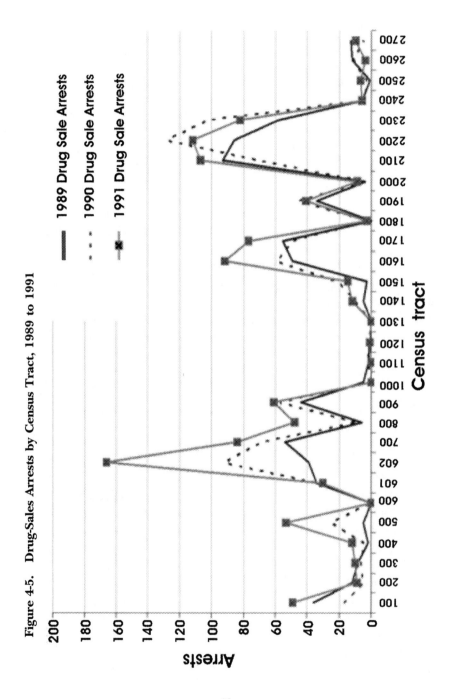

Figure 4-5. Drug-Sales Arrests by Census Tract, 1989 to 1991

Figure 4-6. Kernel Density Surface Map of Drug-Sales Arrests, 1989 to 1991

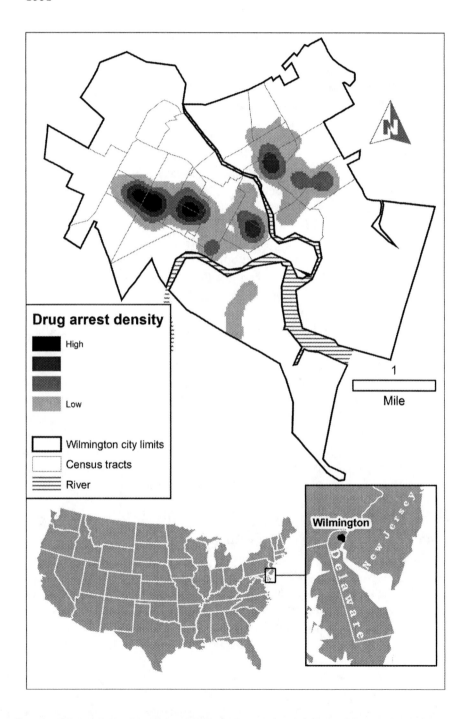

a median age of first use below 15 years. The median age of first drug use excluding alcohol identified in Inciardi's (1995) study was 15.2 years.

In their study of crack users in Miami, Florida, Inciardi and Pottieger (1995) determined that school attendance was not a high priority among the school age crack users. Twenty-two percent of the subjects had dropped out of school. More telling, 89.4% had been expelled or suspended from school. Since the entire sample of 254 youths was below 17 years of age (some as young as 12), school dropout rates will undoubtedly be higher as the sample approaches and exceeds 18 years of age. To obtain money for crack use, these 254 youths were responsible for over 220,000 criminal offenses during the 12 months prior to the interview. The main source of income was from drug sales. Over 61% of the offenses were for illegal drug sales, 11.4% were vice offenses including prostitution, 23.3% were property offenses, and 4.2% were major felonies such as robbery and burglary. It would be difficult to maintain a serious educational career while simultaneously concentrating on a career of crime and drug abuse (Rengert and Wasilchick, 2000).

McCoy et al. (1995) determined that female crack cocaine users over the age of 18 also were not likely to be high school graduates. In the sample of 235 female crack users, 59.7% did not have a high school diploma, 64.5% exchanged sex for money and 24.2% exchanged sex for drugs. Again, these activities are not conducive to a serious formal career.

When we focus directly on employment, Fagan (1993) identified unemployment as an important factor leading many youth to choose to sell illegal drugs in post-industrial cities. As industries close or move from these cities, high-wage low-skill fabrication and assembly jobs also disappear, leaving few if any legitimate alternative employment opportunities of the same caliber. John Ball (1991) determined that drug addicts typically are not legally employed. He describes how they support their drug habits in the informal economy. He found that addicts in New York, Philadelphia, and Baltimore committed an average of 603, 631, and 567 offenses, respectively, each year. This computes to well over one a day. In other words, crime is a routine activity in these drug addicts' daily lives. Finally, Pettiway (1994) in his ethnographic study of addicts in inner city Philadelphia found the vast majority to be unemployed in the formal economy.

These studies illustrate that not only local demand, but also the local availability of labor to sell illegal drugs, may be closely related to the unemployment and school dropout status of an area. Therefore, if one were an illegal drug dealer concerned with maximizing profits from sales to a local clientele, a major consideration would be accessibility of the site to the young, the unemployed, and the post-teens with less than a high school education. This leads to methods of identifying such sites, methods developed in marketing geography.

MARKETING GEOGRAPHY

The retail sale of illegal drugs has principles in common with the sale of legal products. For both, the goal is to make a profit. Illegal operations also have the additional goal of avoiding apprehension. The location of the sales enterprise is a strong factor in the attainment of both goals (Rengert, 1996). Ghosh and McLafferty (1987:2) highlight the importance of spatial location:

> A well-designed location strategy is an integral and important part of corporate strategy for retail firms. Whether selling goods or services, the choice of outlet locations is perhaps the most important decision a retailer has to make. It is through the location that goods and services are made available to potential customers. *Good locations allow ready access, attract large numbers of customers, and increase the potential sales of retail outlets.* (emphasis added)

Seldom have the locations of illegal enterprises been evaluated from this marketing perspective (Eck, 1994). More commonly, the locations are related to the social and economic status of neighborhoods (Davis et al., 1993), and the deterioration of the built environment (Skogan, 1990).

Marketing geographers have identified several strategies for determining optimal locations for retail firms (Davies, 1984). One such strategy is a location-allocation model (Ghosh and McLafferty, 1987). Location-allocation models of retail geography consist of five basic elements:

1. the objective function;

2. demand points;

3. feasible sites;

4. a distance matrix; and,

5. an allocation rule.

In the present study, we used the objective function of maximizing sales volume by minimizing distance to potential customers. The demand points are assumed to be the centroids of census tracts in Wilmington, Delaware. In this initial analysis, we used a "planar model" that assumes feasible sites for illegal drug markets exist everywhere in Wilmington. This assumption is relaxed later in the analysis to mask wealthy housing areas where drug markets are not likely to be established. Computing the distance between the centroids of census tracts in Wilmington formed a distance matrix. The allocation rule is that potential customers are assigned to the census tract that minimizes total distance traveled by potential customers for illegal drugs.

The Location-Allocation Analysis

We began the analysis by determining which census tract is the most centrally located in Wilmington. This was determined by summing the distances between each census tract and all the others in Wilmington (the columns in a distance matrix). The census tract with the smallest sum, tract #1600, is the most centrally located in Wilmington (Figure 4-7).

This tract is the most accessible to the total area if we ignore transportation infrastructure and the distribution of potential customers. Secondly, we determined which census tracts contained the most arrests for illegal drug sales per square kilometer during the years 1989-91. This turned out to be census tract 2200 (see Table 4-1 and Figure 4-7). In other words, if police arrests for drug sales are an indicator of the location of illegal drug sales, then they were more concentrated in census tract 2200 than any other. There also were high concentrations in census tracts 2100, 2300, and 1600.

The above analyses tell us which census tract is the most centrally located in Wilmington and which census tract contains the most arrests for illegal drug sales. They do not tell us where the greatest demand for illegal drugs is likely to be located. We determine this by examining where individuals who are likely to have the greatest demand are located and where they must travel to purchase illegal drugs – if the illegal drug market is located so that, in the aggregate, they have to travel the fewest person-miles to reach this location. From the National Survey on Drug Abuse (U.S. Department of Health and Human Services, 1993), we determine that the demand for illegal drug use is likely to be greatest

Figure 4-7. Labeled Census Tracts: Hot Spots of Drug-Sales Arrests, 1989-1991

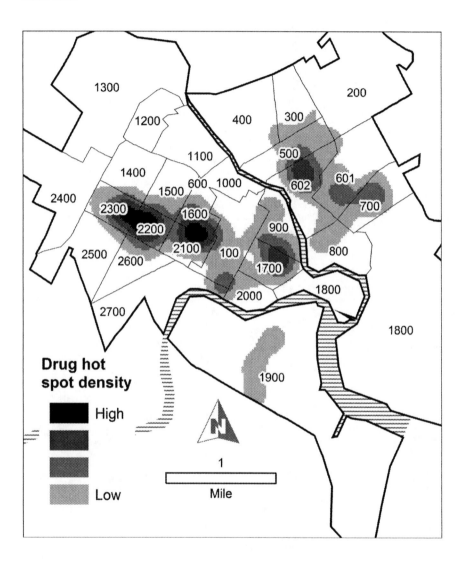

for young people between the ages of 15 and 29, among unemployed individuals and among high school dropouts. When these three factors are combined into a profile of demand for illegal drugs, it is determined that illegal drug users in Wilmington would have to travel the fewest

Table 4-1. Drug Arrests per Square Kilometer in 1989-1991

Census Tract	Area (sq. km.)	Total Drug Arrests	Drug Arrest % by Tract	Arrests (sq. km.)
2200	0.26	320	13.3%	1230.8
2100	0.30	270	11.2%	900.0
2300	0.35	239	9.9%	682.9
1600	0.32	186	7.7%	581.3
1700	0.38	174	7.2%	457.9
602	0.64	284	11.8%	443.8
700	0.55	205	8.5%	372.7
900	0.40	132	5.5%	330.0
500	0.49	69	2.9%	140.8
100	0.79	91	3.8%	115.2
800	0.54	51	2.1%	94.4
601	0.85	77	3.2%	90.6
1500	0.41	36	1.5%	87.8
1400	0.49	24	1.0%	49.0
2000	0.28	13	0.5%	46.4
300	0.47	19	0.8%	40.4
2600	0.45	16	0.7%	35.6
1900	4.44	114	4.7%	25.7
1000	0.28	5	0.2%	17.9
2500	0.76	13	0.5%	17.1
400	1.02	17	0.7%	16.7
2700	0.91	15	0.6%	16.5
200	1.79	21	0.9%	11.7
2400	1.29	12	0.5%	9.3
1100	0.60	4	0.2%	6.7
1200	0.41	1	0.0%	2.4
1800	6.07	4	0.2%	0.7
600	0.01	0	0.0%	0.0
1300	2.25	0	0.0%	0.0
Totals	**27.80**	**2412**	**100%**	

person-miles if the illegal drug market was located in census tract #1600. From Table 4-1, we can see that, correcting for census tract area, tract #1600 has the fourth largest concentration of drug-sale arrests. We now proceed to enhance this basic location-allocation model.

Limitations of the Location-Allocation Model

There are two important limitations of the simple form of the location-allocation model. The first is the assumption of a "planar model," in which any location in the city of Wilmington is a potential site for an illegal drug market. Clearly residents of stable neighborhoods with expensive homes are not likely to tolerate open-air drug markets in their midst (Figure 4-8 shows a winding street in an affluent neighborhood). In fact, even indoor drug sales locations have been sites of confrontations in stable neighborhoods (Lacoya, 1989). Therefore, we

Figure 4-8. A Winding Street in an Affluent Neighborhood in West Wilmington

relaxed this assumption to mask out residential areas such as in Figure 4-8, where the median value of housing was above the average for the city of Wilmington.

The second limitation is the assumption that local addicts will travel anywhere in Wilmington to purchase illegal drugs. Pettiway (1994) determined that most addicts do not travel beyond a mile in their journey to purchase illegal drugs. Therefore, we modified our model with a dummy variable of zero if a census tract center was beyond a mile of another and a one if it was equal to or less than a mile.

We combined these two relaxations of the original model by first excluding from the analysis combinations of census tracts that are more than a mile from each other. Then we used the composite factor model, whereby census tracts containing residential units valued above the median for the city were not considered, and the next most optimal census tract was considered. In this case we no longer used the distance matrix. In its place we used a matrix containing zeros and ones and identified those tracts that were within a mile of the largest number of people that fit our composite profile of potential illegal drug users.

This analysis produced more realistic spatial arrangements than the previous analysis. Figure 4-9 illustrates that there are two clusters of census tracts that are within one mile of the most potential customers as identified by the composite demographic profile and are below the median value of housing for the city of Wilmington. The most advanta-geous location is the area including the contiguous census tracts 2200, 2300, and 1400. These three tracts ranked first, second, and third on our composite profile of potential customers while still containing homes below the median value for the city. The census tracts that ranked fourth and fifth using these same criteria formed a second cluster to the east along state highway 13. They are the contiguous census tracts 601 and 602.

These census tracts identified in our final analysis rank near the top in terms of arrests for the sale of illegal drugs. In fact, each forms the heart of a major spatial cluster of arrests for illegal drug sales in Wilmington. Tract 2200 also is the location of a major interchange on interstate highway I-95. Therefore, it also is expected to serve the non-local commuter traffic funneled into the city.

What this tells us is that the basic location-allocation model can be enhanced by the addition of further information about the drug-using population. Given the young age of many drug users, the limita-

Figure 4-9. Predicted High Drug-Arrest Clusters
(The darker shading indicates predicted high-arrest clusters.)

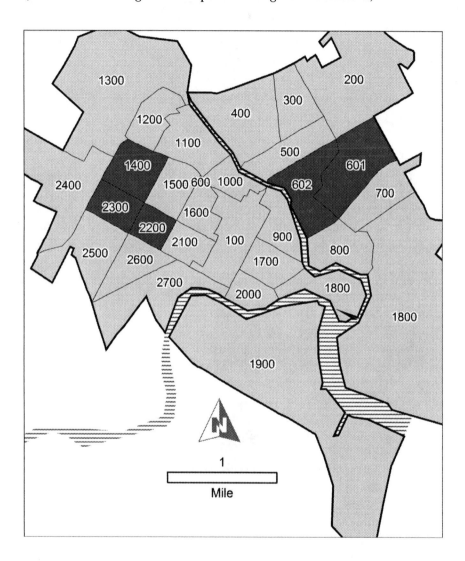

tions on travel are considerable, and the existence of a drug market more than a mile away from their main domicile will often either be unknown to them, or deemed too far to travel. When this enhancement is added into the model, the location-allocation model does an effective job of predicting drug market locations.

SUMMARY

In this chapter we have explored the spatial economics of local drug markets. The geography of drug markets has been examined from the perspective of what we know, from previous research, about the user community. The location-allocation model proved successful in predicting likely areas of drug markets, albeit at the coarse scale of the census tract. The accuracy of the model would appear to reinforce existing knowledge of the behavior patterns of the user community.

The importance of targeting these potential users cannot be overemphasized. They create the market and therefore the profits from illegal drug sales. If addicted, many form a symbiotic relationship with illegal drug dealers, and they weaken the social fabric of a neighborhood through their crime. This, in turn, allows drug dealers to operate more openly. Through geographic market analysis, we attempted to predict in which part of the city it is most profitable to locate these local markets, although not all may have attracted the attention of the police. If these local markets have locational advantages, they may be the forerunners of more noxious open-air drug market places.

From a problem-oriented policing perspective, this becomes the foundation for a more thorough analysis of the drug market prior to the formulation of a plan to resolve the drug problem. As noted earlier, the exact dimensions of the problem are too often ill defined in problem-oriented policing projects. We suggest that the basic analysis demonstrated here acts as one possible starting point, and not the completion, of a drug market analysis. Problem-oriented policing examples are recounted later in this book.

What we have not considered in our analysis to this point is the exact location within these parts of the city, and the relative importance of the demographic and locational variables. We also have not considered factors in the built environment that may aggregate potential drug users spatially on a routine basis. Such environmental features (for example high schools or drug treatment centers) may provide a rich market potential. Finally, we have relied on a rather crude spatial construction by analyzing census tracts. In the following analysis, we use Geographic Information Systems (GIS) and more refined statistical analyses to disentangle these important issues. Specifically, we are attempting to identify problems associated with specific sites in the local community that police, public agencies, and community leaders may address to build more stable, drug-free neighborhoods.

5. ESTABLISHING THE ANALYTIC FRAMEWORK

Note to readers: This chapter and the next describe the statistical analyses that were conducted on the Wilmington data to explore the distribution of drug arrests in the city. By necessity, the text gets a bit technical in some places. This is required because we think our approach is innovative as well as statistically robust. By explaining the techniques and findings in detail, we hope to provide other researchers with the opportunity to replicate this type of study and learn about additional cities. However, we also recognize that some readers may not wish to delve deeply into the statistics. If spatial statistics don't excite you, then a summary of the significant findings can be found in Chapter 7.

In the previous chapter, we used variables associated with the demand for illegal drugs to identify spaces within which illegal drugs are likely to be sold. As we pointed out, the limitations of this type of study included the rather coarse nature of the analysis (at the census tract level). In the present chapter, we will refine this analysis to identify the specific places within these spaces that illegal drug sales are likely to cluster around. These are the sites that theoretically should be attractive to illegal drug dealers. We begin by examining social theories that assist us in identifying these sites. Then we will add characteristics of the physical environment to construct a more complete picture. Especially important are the built environment features that form the anchors of routine activities of potential drug users and the transportation infrastructure that funnels regional customers into the city.

Analytical Model

The analysis is based on several theoretical foundations. The first is the locational theory from marketing geography identified in the previous chapter. This theory uses the concept of a demographic profile of a population to measure local demand for illicit drugs. These measures are derived from past research that identifies the demographic characteristics of drug addicts much as market analysts use demographic profiling to establish market demand for legitimate commodities. We again use variables identified by the Household Survey of Drug Abuse conducted by the U.S. Department of Health and Human Services (1993), which established that drug addicts tend to:

(1) be unemployed in the formal economy;

(2) have low formal income levels; and

(3) be members of minority ethnic groups.

The Household Survey of Drug Abuse established which groups are most likely to use illegal drugs. It is purely descriptive. It did not explain why these demographically defined populations are more likely to use drugs and therefore likely to attract illegal drug dealers to their neighborhoods. For this explanation we must turn to theories developed in criminology. One of the most cited theories centers on a community's ability to work together with the aid of the police to solve problems such as illegal drug dealers in its midst. This "social disorganization" theory (Shaw and McKay, 1942) explains why neighbors may not band together to resist what in the previous chapter were shown to be economically-induced forces. This theory holds that population turnover and heterogeneity make it difficult for neighbors to cooperate. The following authors have described and refined this theory.

Social disorganization is described by Bursik (1988:521) as follows:

> In its purest form, social disorganization refers to the inability of local communities to realize the common values of their residents or solve commonly experienced problems. . . . Population turnover and heterogeneity are assumed to increase the likelihood of disorganization for the following reasons:
>
> (1) Institutions pertaining to internal control are difficult to establish when many residents are "uninterested in communities they hope to leave at the first opportunity" (Kornhauser, 1978:78).
> (2) The development of primary relationships that result in informal structures of social control is less likely when local networks are in a continual state of flux (see Berry and Kasarda, 1977).
> (3) Heterogeneity impedes communication and thus obstructs the quest to solve common problems and reach common goals (Kornhauser, 1978:75).

Therefore, according to social disorganization theory, population turnover and heterogeneity make it more difficult for residents to resist dealers who wish to establish a drug market in their neighborhoods. Dunlap (1992) identified the impact of illegal drugs on intracity social networks more directly. He points out that drug use decreases trust among community members because the drug users' focus is on their own problems rather than community concerns.

In addition to these factors identified by Bursik (1988) and Dunlap (1992), we also expect to find social disorganization in communities dominated by single-parent families. Johnson et al. (2000:167) describe this as a typical situation in drug-infested, inner city communities:

> A typical household might be headed by a single mother (or often grandmother) living on welfare, without a legal job and having no prospects for legal jobs due to poor jobs skills and a heavy burden of child care responsibilities. Sometimes the household head's chances of employment are further restricted by demands of regular drug use. Children growing up in such households often do not know anyone who works at a legal job. . . . They rarely complete high school and do not learn the basic skills (literacy, numeracy, punctuality, ability to take directions, and mainstream norms of interaction) needed to find and keep legal employment as adults.

Dunlap (1995) places men in this scenario as well. He describes the impact of illegal drug dealing within the household of the dealer, including the possibility of domestic violence. According to social disorganization theory, illegal drug markets are much more likely to locate where there is social disorganization within as well as outside the family, because in such locations active organized resistance to drug dealing is less likely to materialize (Johnson et al., 2000).

However, not all scholars feel that communities must be closely knit together to control or resist illegal drug dealers in their neighborhoods. Morenoff et al. (2001) point out that social organization is not sufficient or even necessary to control crime. They cite Pattillo-McCoy (1999), who discovered in a black middle-class community in Chicago that, while dense local ties promote social integration, such bonds also foster the growth of networks that impede efforts to rid the neighborhood of drug- and gang-related crime. In other communities, Sampson et al. (1999) have found that shared expectations for social control can exist despite the absence of thick ties among neighbors. They coined the term "social efficacy" to describe such behavior.

In the present research in Wilmington, it will be determined whether illicit drug markets can become established in neighborhoods that have the characteristics of well-organized communities or, conversely, whether illicit drug markets fail to become established in neighborhoods that have the characteristics of disorganized communities. Measures of social disorganization used in this analysis are:

(1) high population turnover;

(2) high levels of vacant properties at the block-group level;

(3) a high proportion of families in which children under five are living with a single parent;

(4) a predominance of renter- as opposed to owner-occupied housing; and,

(5) a high percentage of minority residents.

The second variable (high levels of vacant properties) may explain why illegal drug markets do not become established in all socially disorganized neighborhoods. If there is a high level of vacant homes in a neighborhood, we would expect local demand to decline as local residents leave the area. This is because occupancy may drop below the threshold level required to keep a local drug market in business.

If local demand for illegal drugs drops below the threshold level of profitability, then the illegal drug market must rely on factors that bring potential drug users into the community rather than on the local residents. These factors are related to facilities used on a routine basis by potential drug users, including young people, the unemployed, school dropouts, etc. These ideas are derived from "routine activity" theory, which was first formulated by Cohen and Felson (1979). According to routine activity theory, crime is likely to take place when a motivated offender comes into contact in time and space with a suitable target that is not guarded capably. In other words, drug markets are likely to appear near facilities in our cities that aggregate many potential targets (customers) for drug dealers on a routine basis in an area is not adequately guarded by place managers, local neighbors and/or the police.

Urban Facilities Linked to Potential Drug Sales

Facilities used on a routine basis by young people in Wilmington include charter high schools. Roncek and Lobosco (1983) found crime clustered around high schools. This finding was replicated by Roncek and

Faggiani (1985). Rengert and Chakravorty (1995) found arrests for drug sales clustered more within than outside drug-free zones around schools in central Philadelphia. These studies lead us to expect that crime and drug dealing will cluster around schools. However, due to desegregation orders, Wilmington does not have a centralized high school, but it does have charter high schools within the city limits. Charter schools differ from neighborhood public schools in having discretion over which students are admitted. They can attract students from throughout the city. In contrast to neighborhood public schools, whose students are likely to walk from home, charter school students are more likely to be bused or driven to school. Yet, both types of schools aggregate youths who are potential drug users. Therefore, we expect illegal drug dealers to establish markets near schools that bring together students 15 years of age or older.

Older addicts are expected to routinely use bars and liquor stores to supplement their addiction lifestyles with alcohol. A series of studies (Roncek and Bell, 1981; Roncek and Pravatiner, 1989; Roncek and Maier, 1991) has established that crime tends to be more likely on blocks containing taverns and bars. Engstad (1975), Maier (1989), Hope (1985) and Sherman et al. (1989) also found liquor establishments to be associated with hot spots of crime. Finally, Wieczorek and Coyle (1996) differentiated between liquor establishments where the liquor was consumed on site from those where the liquor was taken from the premises to be consumed. They found significantly more crime associated with establishments where the liquor is consumed off premises. It is not clear whether the crime is due to the effects of alcohol or due to the clustering of potential criminals and/or victims in and around these establishments, as suggested by routine activity theory. In the present analysis, liquor stores where liquor is consumed off premises are analyzed separately from bars and taverns where liquor is consumed on premises. This is an important distinction since tavern owners and employees are expected to be capable guardians on their premises, while liquor stores are not responsible for the sidewalks, local parks, and vacant lots outside their premises.

Check-cashing stores and pawnshops also are expected to be used routinely by low-income people on public assistance who may have a high potential for illegal drug use. In describing a low-income neighborhood in central Philadelphia, Elijah Anderson (1998:77) notes the uses of these facilities:

> There are businesses that cater mostly to the criminal class, such as pawnshops. . . . Pawnshops are in a sense banks for thieves; they are places where stolen goods can be traded for cash, few questions asked. Check-cashing exchanges, which continue to be a common sight, also ask few questions, but they charge exorbitant fees for cashing a check.

These are the types of facilities that are useful to illicit drug users, who must turn goods and welfare checks into cash without delay.

Finally, homeless shelters and drug/alcohol treatment centers are expected to be used routinely by individuals with addiction problems. Not all residents of homeless shelters are drug addicts. However, drug addiction may be a cause of homelessness (Rengert, 1996). Indirect evidence that homeless shelters are routinely used by some illegal drug abusers is found in research conducted by Metraux and Culhane (2004). They studied 48,424 New York City residents who were released from New York State prisons in 1995-1998. Over half of these individuals had served time for drug offenses. Upon release, 11.4% entered a New York City homeless shelter and 32.8% were imprisoned again within two years. Residence in a shelter for homeless persons increased the risk of subsequent incarceration. The homeless shelters clearly bring together at one location individuals with a higher potential for drug use and sales than the general population.

Gelberg et al. (1988) and Snow et al. (1989) also documented the criminality and drug use of homeless individuals. These studies illustrate that homeless shelters and drug treatment centers bring potential drug users into a neighborhood that might not otherwise house a threshold level of potential drug users.

On the other hand, drug distributors probably do not want to locate near fire and police stations. These facilities have capable guardians coming, going and located at or near them. For example, fire stations commonly have doors open and men working on equipment near the public sidewalk. It is not likely that these public employees would tolerate illicit activity near their facility.

There is a final feature of the environment that is used routinely by regional residents who are potential customers for inner-city drug dealers. These are transportation hubs that funnel traffic into Wilmington. The most important is I-95, a limited access interstate highway that has exits within Wilmington. We expect drug dealers to establish markets at or near these exits to sell to regional customers funneled into the city (Eck, 1994).

A second group of public transportation facilities that funnel regional traffic into Wilmington are the Amtrak train station and regional bus stations. These stations disgorge many passengers from outside the city who are potential customers for illegal drug dealers. Finally, major highways bring traffic into and throughout Wilmington. Eck (1994) found that outdoor drug markets in San Diego clustered along major highways of that city. In Wilmington, we define major highways as traffic arteries of four lanes or more of continuous roadway (not counting parking spaces) that move traffic throughout the city. These four lane highways provide a traffic volume that contains potential customers for drug dealers.

A combination of known socio-economic and demographic characteristics, with proximity to certain built environment features (positive and negative), plus accessibility to cars and public transportation, should create the appropriate conditions for a drug market. We expect different combinations of the above factors to be associated with drug sales. For example, in order to reach threshold conditions necessary to remain in business, if a site is *not* located near a transportation hub or a built facility used routinely by potential drug users, then it must be in a neighborhood containing socio-economic and demographically identified individuals who are potential drug users. These are the ideas tested in the following analysis.

The Model of Drug Sales Potential

The analytical task is to combine all these variables into a single model of Drug Sales Potential. The variables identified by the various theories discussed above are grouped together for analysis so that the relative strength or usefulness of the various theories in explaining where local drug markets are established can be compared. We term the demographic variables that measure social disorganization and local demand *susceptibility* variables. Facilities associated with the routine activities of potential drug users that attract them into a neighborhood are termed *activity* variables. Finally, the transportation infrastructure that funnels regional customers into the city is termed the *accessibility* factors. The null hypothesis is as follows:

Drug Sales Potential of a neighborhood =
f (susceptibility, activity, accessibility)

Only one of these factors needs to be evident to establish threshold conditions necessary to form a drug market in a neighborhood. However, if two or all the factors are evident, surplus profits may allow competing dealers to locate in the neighborhood, leading to a profitable drug mart or cluster of competing sellers enjoying agglomeration economies.

Spatial Analysis

We now turn our attention to the mechanisms of the spatial analysis of the drug sales potential model. A problem facing spatial analysts is how to combine point, line, and polygon features. A polygon feature is any feature that has spatial extent in more than one dimension. For example, a point has no spatial extent; a line has spatial extent in only one dimension, while a polygon has spatial extent in two dimensions. A polygon is usually delimited by boundaries that do not exist in point or line features. For example, census data are in the form of a polygon.

A problem with census data in the form of a polygon is that the variable being mapped is assumed to be uniformly distributed across the polygon. For example, if we have a measure of unemployment within a census tract, it can only be assumed that the unemployment rate is the same across the whole census tract. It is the equivalent of an average figure.

Point and line features are different. We do not assume that their influence is constant over space as is the case within a census polygon. For example, hubs of routine activities, such as liquor stores or homeless shelters, are points in space. Customers moving toward this point come from a variety of directions that converge on the entrance to the facility (a point in space). Therefore, the impact of the point will have an aerial extent beyond this built feature, which declines with distance from the facility as the users disperse throughout the city. For example, an illegal drug dealer could contact a customer of a liquor store anywhere outside the store on the path taken by the customer to or from the store. However, the closer to the store, the denser the aerial agglomeration of customers will be as they converge on the entrance. If the drug dealer hopes to attract customers from the liquor store, it makes sense to stay near the store and near the "action."

In order to determine the aerial extent of the impact of a point feature, the concept of "revealed activities" is used in this analysis (Rushton, 1969). A revealed activity is a concept used to measure an activity that cannot be measured directly. In other words, we cannot directly measure the relative profitability of a location to a drug dealer since we do not have access to their records (if any are kept). On the other hand, revealed activity tells us that the market location would not be active if threshold conditions of profitability were not met at that location (Hough and Edmunds, 1997). Furthermore, if excess profits are evident, competing sellers will be attracted to the location and will operate as closely as possible to the advantaged location. Therefore, the relative density of drug-sales arrests can measure the revealed profitability of a location or small area. By relative density, we mean more or less dense than an established norm.

The norm used to establish spatial concentration of illicit drug sales is the "masked" city of Wilmington. The reason a masked city is used is so that we are comparing areas where there is some potential for illegal drug sales. Areas of the city where there are few, if any, drug-sales arrests are removed from this part of the analysis. This also solves the problem that facilities tend to be located near the center of the city. Drug-sales activity also is less likely in the outlying areas of the city. Rather than measuring centrality, the relative spatial concentration of drug-sales arrests in areas with some potential for drug sales is measured. The masked city has a greater density of drug-sales arrests than the city as a whole. Therefore, the concentration of drug-sales arrests around a facility will be compared to this greater density than if the entire city were used. The question is whether or not drug-sales arrests around a facility or neighborhood are more or less dense spatially than this norm. The measure used to establish this comparison is termed a *Location Quotient* (discussed below).

The question now turns to how the area is circumscribed around a point or line feature for use in the Location Quotient (LQ). This can be somewhat arbitrary. However, there is reason to argue that a city block is an important spatial extent in most residents' minds (Smith et. al., 2000; Robinson, 2003; Roncek and Bell, 1981). In Wilmington, a block varies in length, but in general it is approximately 400 feet. Therefore, multiples of 400 feet are used in this analysis to define "buffers" around point and line features. In other words, we examine the density of incidents at distance bands (buffers) of 0 to 400 feet, 400 to 800 feet, and so on, as doughnuts expanding outward from the urban feature under examination. By trial, we examine each buffer beginning with four hundred feet to determine which contains the densest spatial agglomeration of drug-sales arrests. We also are interested in whether each succeeding buffer out from a feature decreases in the density of drug-sales arrests in a monotonic manner. That is, each succeeding buffer outward is expected to have a lower density of drug-sales arrests than its inner neighbor. In this manner, the buffers describe the spatial influence (if any) of a point or line feature in the analysis.

These methods (detailed later) allow us to examine small areas that are not dependent on census definitions for their boundaries. In other words, GIS allows us to create new geographies defined by the buffers of point and line features overlaid with each other and block groups. This does not correct for the problem that the census variables are assumed to be uniformly distributed across block groups. However, it allows the block groups to be redefined by additional features that are not assumed to be uniformly distributed. In this manner, GIS allows a more refined analysis than when it is restricted to census definitions of areas. As a result, we increase the spatial precision of this analysis over that conducted in the previous chapter.

DATA DESCRIPTION

In this section the exact form of the data identified above is discussed. Three general types of data are used: police data on arrests, census data on residents, and geographical data on the locations of crime generators and criminal attractors (Brantingham and Brantingham, 1995a).

Police Data on Arrests

The Delaware Statistical Analysis Center provided nine years (1989-1997, both years inclusive) of arrest and call-for-service data for the study area. The arrest data files included information on time, location, and type of drug offense. Table 5-1 details the arrest information.

The focus of the analysis is to identify the factors associated with the location and formation of drug markets so that problem-oriented

Table 5-1. Drug-Related Arrests in the Study Area

Year	Arrests for drug possession, entire city	Arrests for drug sales, entire city	Total drug arrests, entire city	Arrests for drug possession, masked city	Arrests for sales, masked city	Total drug arrests, masked city
1989	615	610	1,225	591	580	1,171
1990	541	779	1,320	529	760	1,289
1991	571	1,028	1,599	557	1,001	1,558
1992	452	751	1,203	443	737	1,180
1993	312	701	1,013	294	691	985
1994	329	586	915	321	569	890
1995	346	702	1,048	332	685	1,017
1996	267	641	908	264	637	901
1997	287	675	962	279	668	947
Totals	3,720	6,473	10,193	3,610	6,328	9,938

policing tactics may be identified to counter these forces. We therefore are not interested in all drug-related arrests, but only those arrests that are related to drug sales or distribution (and not simple possession). The data in Table 5-1 show that the drug sales-related arrests numbered about 700 on average per year. The analysis focuses both on the entire city and the masked city.

Census Data and Susceptibility

The details of the census data used in the models are listed below in Table 5-2. These data form the basis for operationalizing the demographic profile of local demand, social disorganization and social efficacy. Together, they form the measures of *susceptibility*. These are the conditions that make specific places economically attractive and socially vulnerable or susceptible to drug dealers. These also are the conditions that result from the establishment of a drug market in a neighborhood, which may lead to social disorganization.

The census variables used refer to these characteristics of the population and neighborhood at the census block-group level. A census block group is smaller than a census tract. A census tract contains about

Table 5-2. Census Variable Definitions

VARIABLE	DEFINITION
Median Income	The median income in a block group.
Percent Female-headed Households with Children	Computed by dividing the total number of families in a block group by the total number of single-parent, female-headed households with at least one child under the age of 5 years in the block group.
Percent Renter-occupied Housing	Computed by dividing the total number of occupied housing units in a block group into the number of non-vacant housing units occupied by renting tenants in the block group.
Percent Males Unemployed	Computed by dividing the number of non-disabled males over the age of 16 in a block group into the number of unemployed non-disabled males over the age of 16 years in the block group.
Percent Minority Population	Computed by dividing the total number of residents in a block group into the number of non-white residents in the block group.
Vacancy Rate	Computed by dividing the total number of housing units in a block group into the number of vacant housing units in the block group.
Percent of Residents Who Did Not Live in Present Home 5 Years Ago	Computed by dividing the total number of residents in a block group into the number of residents in the block group who did not live in their present home 5 years ago.

4,000 residents. There are four or five block groups within a census tract, each containing about 1,000 residents. Census block groups are assumed to be more homogeneous than census tracts since they are smaller in size. There is the question of what came first, drug markets or socially disorganized neighborhoods? This is an issue that we recognize remains to be disentangled in the future.

Geographic Data, Accessibility and Activity

The final form of data used is composed of elements of geography. It is the group of spatial artifacts and anchors that create the conditions of accessibility and activity.

Drug markets are expected to be more successful in areas of easy access, such as those areas located along major roads, at public transportation interchanges where one must change from one mode of transportation to another, and at the exits from interstate highways (I-95 in this case). A database of accessibility was created that is composed of a set of map coverages of I-95 (with the exit/entry points identified), the entire road system in the city of Wilmington (in which the major roads were identified after consultation with Wilmington police and our own field observations), and points identifying the locations of bus stations and the train station. These coverages form our accessibility database.

Certain built environment features act as attractors or repellants of drug-sales activity. This concept builds on Brantingham and Brantingham's (1995a) definition of crime generators and criminal attractors. The following types of built environment features are expected to attract illicit drug dealers:

(1)   check-cashing stores,

(2)   liquor stores,

(3)   homeless shelters,

(4)   social service program locations,

(5)   taverns, and

(6)   pawn shops.

It is not obvious, from a theoretical perspective, what effects (attracting or repelling) would be manifested around courts and the federal building, fire stations, police stations, and schools. There are good reasons to suspect that this second set of artifacts could, depending on the situation, be either attractive or repellant. The schools argument was discussed with reference to the drug-free schools policy. As a result, digital coverages of the following additional built environment features were created:

(1)   courts and the federal building,

(2)   fire stations,

(3)   police stations, and

(4)   schools.

The methods used to determine the most relevant of these spatial variables are discussed in a later section.

Delimitation of Geography

The city of Wilmington contains 80 census block groups. This is not a large city by any means, but interestingly, as the primary city in a small state, Wilmington appears to exhibit many of the characteristics of much larger cities, but on a smaller scale. For instance, the city has a clearly identifiable downtown with high-rise buildings and a downtown mall area, and equally clearly identifiable areas of population congestion and minority concentration around the downtown. Toward the edges of the city, to the north and west in particular, are affluent white-dominated suburbs. To the south and east is the Wilmington Port area, which occupies a large geographical area, but is very sparsely populated. Figure 5-1 shows the block groups of the city.

LOCATION QUOTIENTS AND THE SELECTION OF SPATIAL PARAMETERS

Routine activity theory implies that built environment features act as anchors that attract (or possibly repel) potential drug customers on a routine basis. It is important to determine whether this is true, and more important, to what extent this is true for each specific type of feature. The goals are twofold: first, to identify the spatial extent to which specific features are associated with a concentration of drug dealers. That is, does the feature affect only the block on which it is located, or two blocks around it, or some other spatial arrangement (such as a doughnut effect)? A second goal is to identify those feature types that are the most attractive locations for drug markets, and thereby to retain only those features for the final modeling exercises. In other words, the objective is to identify those features that have drug-sales arrests clustered about them. A technique for quantifying the degree of attraction of a specific feature is the *Location Quotient* (LQ). It is a simple measure used extensively in regional science and urban economics, and has been previously applied in the criminal justice field (Brantingham and Brantingham, 1995b; Robinson, 2003). The LQ for an individual parcel within a large number of parcels is calculated by

Figure 5-1.   Block Groups of the Study Area (masked city)

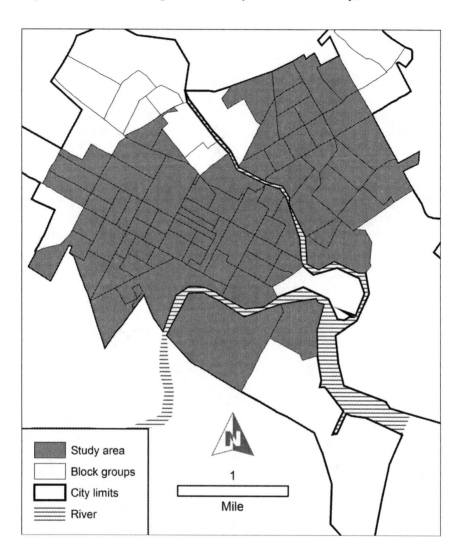

measuring the extent to which a given distribution of events (which may be crime points or trade volumes) is concentrated inside the parcel, assuming that the average intensity of events over all parcels is the expected distribution. In this case LQ is given by:

$$LQ = \textit{Density of drug-sales arrests around selected feature} \;/$$
$$\textit{density of drug-sales arrests in the masked city}$$

When the LQ for a given parcel defined as a one-block radius around a group of specific features (say check-cashing stores) is greater than 1, the implication is that the density of drug-sales arrests around check-cashing stores is higher than the density of drug-sales arrests in the masked city. For a LQ to be a significant factor, and to avoid drawing conclusions based on a single possibly aberrant year, the LQ should be consistently greater than 1 throughout the study period. This is the reason LQs are computed for each of the nine years for each variable analyzed. If LQs vary widely, jumping from below 1 to above 1 (or vice-versa) over the years, the evidence is that there is no consistent reason to believe that the facility attracts drug dealers. Rather, some other factor may have appeared near the facility, or new facilities may have appeared in high or low drug dealing areas of the city. Again, the ideal situation is when the LQs are consistently above or below one for all the years analyzed for any given facility.

Spatial Rules for the Location Quotients

The primary decision to be taken before calculating LQs for the study area hinges on the spatial rules that would be used to identify zones of inclusion around the selected built environment feature types. The built environment features are separated into two general types – those that increase the potential for drug sales because of better access to regional customers, and those that create opportunities for drug sales because they are the anchors for routine activities of potential drug users. The following are the rules used to determine the spatial extent of the impact of a feature on the concentration of drug-sales arrests and the reasoning behind the use of these rules.

Access Features

Interstate 95 exits. The present analysis deviates from the accepted practice of using the complete interstate highway as a possible location for drug sales. Since drug sales involve a transaction between at least two stationary individuals, it is highly improbable that a dealer would undertake sales on the highway itself (except in the rare case of transactions within automobiles where arrests cannot easily be made). Moreover, areas that are immediately adjacent to highways may appear to be possible transaction zones on two-dimensional maps, but even the most casual observer of speeding automobiles knows that such zones are physically unapproachable, and therefore unsuitable for any transaction. Therefore interstate interchanges are selected for analysis; more specifically exits from I-95. It is simple to create a zone around the interchange itself, but that too is unlikely to reflect reality. Drug transactions are most likely to take place at some distance from the physical beginning of an exit – a distance at which the highway traffic meets the regular city traffic. The solution is to create annular rings or doughnuts around highway exits. The question that arose was: what specific distance range is the most likely zone for drug sales?

Our estimate of the length of a city block in Wilmington is 400 feet (used for every feature type below), and what we needed to know was: between which two blocks are drug sales most likely? LQs were calculated for three distance ranges: two to three blocks, two to four blocks, and three to four blocks (since the first block is not conducive to drug transactions because cars are leaving the interstate and cannot stop). The results of these LQ calculations are shown in Figure 5-2 (also see Table 5-3, where all the access criteria and covered area are listed).

From the analysis, it is clear that the 1,200-1,600 foot zone (or the three- to four-block doughnut) is where drug sales are most concentrated. Note that the LQs in all three zones are very high. At its peak, for the 1,200-1,600 foot zone, in 1992, the LQ is over 5; this implies that for that zone for that year the density of drug-sales arrests was five times higher than the region as a whole.

Major roads. Major roads are defined as those four lane or more arteries that are used by people entering or leaving Wilmington, or that are heavily used within the city. The specific major roads were identified with the help of Wilmington Police after a drive-through with their assistance. A buffer of one city block, or 400 feet, is used to create the zone of inclusion around major roads. The 400 foot buffer around major roads covered almost 55% of the study area, despite which the LQs for major roads still averaged around 1.5 (see Table 5-3). Since it is less than 2, major roads are not considered in the remainder of this analysis.

Major Transit Nodes. Major transit nodes are those points where it is possible to change from one form of public transportation to

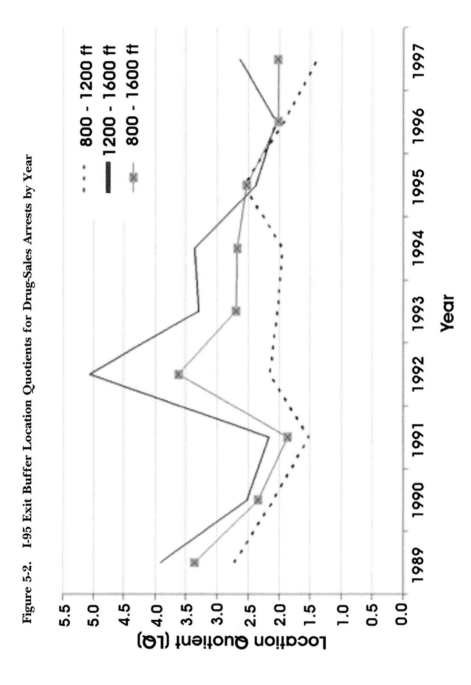

Figure 5-2. I-95 Exit Buffer Location Quotients for Drug-Sales Arrests by Year

Table 5-3. Accessibility Buffers and their Coverage of the Study Area

Type	Buffer Distance (in feet)	Coverage (of study area)
Interstate 95	1,200 – 1,600	4.5%
Major Roads	400	54.8%
Major Transit Nodes	400	0.9%

another, such as from a bus to a train (and vice-versa), or from a bus to another bus. Only three such points were identified in the study area (two bus stations and one train station), where the buffers covered less than 1% of the entire study area. The LQs for this feature type vary widely (from less than 1 in the early 1990s to over 3 by the mid-1990s: see Figure 5-3). This wide fluctuation over time does not lead us to believe that these features are related to illegal drug sales. However, since the value of the location quotient for all years combined is over 2, our criteria have been met and these features are included in the statistical analysis.

Activity Features

Again, only those features that have an LQ above 2 are included in the remainder of the analysis. A LQ of 2 means that drug-sales arrests are clustered twice as much in the buffer around this facility than they are in the "masked city" as a whole. Theoretically, one would expect the clustering of arrests to decline monotonically with distance from a facility that attracted drug dealers. On the other hand, one would expect the clustering of arrests to increase with distance if a facility repelled drug dealers. Therefore, LQs were computed for three buffers around each facility that are approximately multiples of a city block in Wilmington: 400 feet, 400 to 800 feet, and 800 to 1,200 feet around a facility. A 1,000 foot buffer was included around schools to test whether the "drug-free school" laws have a measurable effect.

Table 5-4 lists the LQ in each buffer around each facility. As expected, the spatial clustering of drug-sales arrests is very low around fire stations and the court buildings. Notice that the density increases with distance from these facilities, but never goes much above 1 within the three blocks surrounding each facility. The LQ for pawn shops is

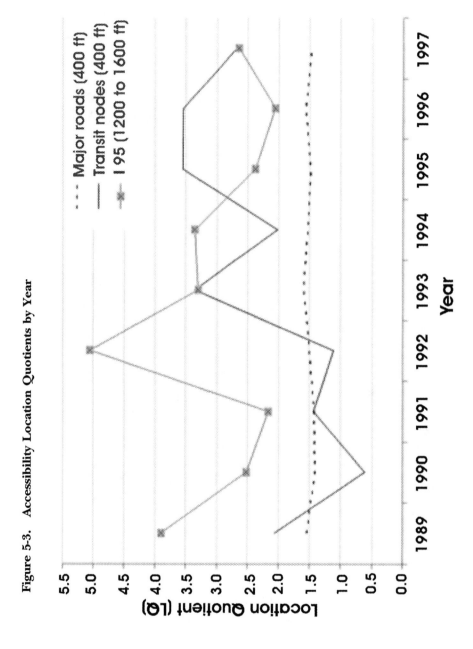

Figure 5-3. Accessibility Location Quotients by Year

Table 5-4. Location Quotients of Activity Buffers

OPPORTUNITY BUFFERS	LOCATION QUOTIENT
400-ft Schools	1.19
800-ft Schools	1.04
1000-ft Schools	0.92
1200-ft Schools	0.58
400-ft Taverns	2.30
800-ft Taverns	1.94
1200-ft Taverns	1.71
400-ft Liquor Stores	2.42
800-ft Liquor Stores	1.66
1200-ft Liquor Stores	1.40
400-ft Check Cashing	3.00
800-ft Check Cashing	2.48
1200-ft Check Cashing	2.06
400-ft Pawn Shop	0.10
800-ft Pawn Shop	1.29
1200-ft Pawn Shop	1.54
400-ft Police Station	1.61
800-ft Police Station	1.49
1200-ft Police Station	1.31
400-ft Court	0.48
800-ft Court	0.65
1200-ft Court	0.95
400-ft Fire Station	0.86
800-ft Fire Station	0.87
1200-ft Fire Station	1.03
400-ft Homeless Shelter	2.93
800-ft Homeless Shelter	3.17
1200-ft Homeless Shelter	2.75
400-ft Social Service Center	1.36
800-ft Social Service Center	2.03
1200-ft Social Service Center	1.83

very low on the first block and never approaches 2 for the other buffers outward. Finally, schools and the police station have total LQs well below 2, although they decrease with distance. In the case of the police station, the larger than expected LQ may be an artifact of the fact that many police officers make arrests for drug sales at the police station if evidence comes in that was not available at the point of arrest. Therefore, police stations often have arrest counts that are higher than normal. In Wilmington, however, the police station location quotients are generally below 2. Since none of these facilities had an LQ above 2 when all years are combined, they are not included in the following analysis. The other facilities in Table 5-4 have LQs above 2 on the first block surrounding them. With the exception of homeless shelters and social service agencies, the density of drug-sales arrests decreases with distance from the facility in a monotonic manner. Both homeless shelters and social service agencies have densities that are higher in the second buffer out (the second block from the facility). It is possible that the staff of these facilities partially control the block on which the facility is located.

It was expected that the strongest effects around the features in Table 5-4 would be within one block (or 400 feet) surrounding them (Roncek and Maier, 1991; Wieczorek and Coyle, 1996). In the case of check-cashing stores, liquor stores and taverns, the expectation clearly was that drug sales would be higher in their proximity. The LQs for these three features are shown in Figure 5-4. As expected, all features generally have LQs significantly higher than 2, except check-cashing stores in the early 1990s. This may be a result of changes in the small number of facilities in certain instances. Note that in Table 5-5 the number of check-cashing stores jumps from 1 in 1992 to 5 in 1993 (that is when the LQ also goes over 1).[1] The area covered by these features together amounts to around 20% of the study area.

Schools, pawn shops, courthouses, police stations and fire stations all had LQs near or below 1 for all years combined. The case of schools in Wilmington will be discussed later. Pawn shops in Wilmington do not seem to attract drug dealers since the LQs for the area around them is near or below 1 for all years. There is no good explanation for this finding. Discussions with Wilmington officials (Bostrom, 2000) indicated that the explanation might be that the pawn shops have a close working relationship with the police and, as a result, may not be used by drug addicts on a routine basis. In the case of police and fire

Figure 5-4.   Activity Location Quotients

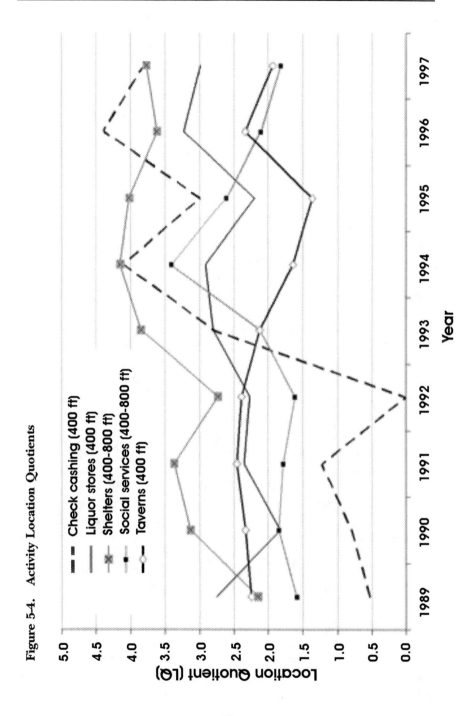

Table 5-5. Number of Activity Locations

TYPE	NUMBER OF PLACES								
	1989	1990	1991	1992	1993	1994	1995	1996	1997
Check Cashing	1	1	1	1	5	5	6	6	6
Liquor Stores	60	60	59	57	57	58	49	45	46
Shelters	6	6	6	6	6	6	6	6	6
Social Service	8	8	8	8	9	9	10	10	10
Taverns	41	41	33	35	33	36	30	32	24

stations and the court buildings, expectations are that they would not attract drug dealers since they have capable guardians coming and going throughout the day. In fact, the LQs for these features are generally below 1, as expected, and as a result they have not been used in the remainder of the analysis.

Shelters and Social Service Centers. We expected that around these two special feature types, the factors leading to increased drug sales and decreased drug sales would play out in interesting ways, with unusual spatial consequences. Immediately around a homeless shelter or social service center, drug dealers would have difficulty operating because of the extra security and scrutiny. In the case of homeless shelters, clients are not allowed to spend the night if they have illegal drugs in their possession. Therefore, there will be an incentive to not purchase drugs on the block in which the facility is located. In fact, Turner (1969) discovered that delinquents in Philadelphia also tended to avoid the block of their residence to avoid recognition. To predict the location of the offender's home from the spatial pattern of his offenses, Rossmo (2000) uses a buffer around the home because crime is less likely to occur in that area. In short, there is reason to believe that drug offenders will avoid purchasing drugs on a block where a facility that is responsible for their behavior is located.

However, since the clients of these services are potential drug purchasers, drug sellers would seek to sell as close to the feature as possible, but not immediately next to it. In other words, we expected an annular or doughnut shaped zone of high drug sales around these features. A one- to two-block doughnut (400 to 800 foot zone) is used for the LQ calculations that are reported in Figure 5-4 (also see Tables

5-5 and 5-6 for more information on these features). It is easy to see that the intensity of drug sales around both features is high, and especially in the case of homeless shelters, drug sales are very high, approaching and even exceeding LQs of 4.

There are two special cases that merit additional discussion. We wanted to study the influence of churches on drug sales, though we were unsure as to what their effect would be. However, we quickly realized that the category of "church" or a place of worship contains such a heterogeneity of features – from cathedrals to store fronts – that it would be impossible to treat all of them under the same label. Since we had no good reason for creating different rules for different "churches," we decided that it was best to avoid confusing the analysis with this feature type altogether. The second special case was schools, which we did study using not only increments of 400 feet, but also the 1,000 feet "drug free school zone" limit. We found that the LQs for schools, using the 1,000 feet buffer, were generally very close to 1 and usually a little less than 1 (note that Wilmington sends its high school students to schools outside Wilmington for desegregation reasons).

Only charter high schools exist within the city. Charter schools are selective with regard to which students are enrolled. Some charter schools select high academic achievers; others select by area of concentration or specialization, such as science and technology, the fine arts, or foreign affairs. The selectivity in admitting these students, as well as the fact that most students are bused or driven to school, may explain

Table 5-6. Changing Size of Area within Activity Buffers

Type	Buffer Distance	Area 1989	Area 1990	Area 1991	Area 1992	Area 1993	Area 1994	Area 1995	Area 1996	Area 1997
Check Cashing	400	0.3%	0.3%	0.3%	0.3%	1.6%	1.6%	1.8%	1.8%	1.8%
Liquor Stores	400	14.2%	14.2%	14.8%	13.6%	13.5%	13.9%	11.4%	10.5%	11.1%
Shelters	400–800	5.3%	5.3%	5.3%	5.3%	5.3%	5.3%	5.3%	5.3%	5.3%
Social Service	400–800	6.5%	6.5%	6.5%	6.5%	7.5%	7.5%	8.3%	8.3%	8.3%
Taverns	400	10.7%	10.7%	10.8%	9.5%	9.5%	9.1%	8.9%	8.7%	8.5%

why drug dealers are not attracted to them. Buses act much like a cocoon sheltering the students from outside influences until they reach the school grounds. Drug dealers hanging around the area, but outside the school property, would not encounter many potential customers. As a result, schools had location quotients near one and are not among the features we have analyzed.

Location quotients are easy to calculate and provide strong evidence that some features of the urban mosaic are crime attractors or crime generators (Brantingham and Brantingham, 1995a) in terms of drug-sales arrests. The strength of the approach used here is that location quotient analysis can demonstrate clustering that is supported by theoretical findings. The limitation is in the lack of integration of different features: in other words, each urban feature must be examined in isolation from the rest of the environment. We resolve this issue in the next sections.

Integrated Spatial Models

The LQs discussed above appear to provide solid evidence in support of the theoretical approach underlying this analysis – that the built environment causes spatial variation in the distribution of drug sales. However, this support may be illusory since the second part of our argument is that no single type of built environment feature causes drug sales to concentrate near it, but that a combination of factors is responsible. These factors include population susceptibility as well as a number of other built environment features (of access and activity) that result in the spatial variation in drug sales. Consider the fact that in 1997 the 400-foot space around check-cashing stores saw drug sales intensity that was more than three times higher than in the masked city. Can we conclude then that the check-cashing stores alone have caused this intensity of drug sales? We cannot, because we do not know anything about the susceptibility of the region (the population age, income, racial composition etc.), nor about the proximity of other built environment features (liquor stores, shelters, etc.) to the check-cashing stores. In order to separate out these individual effects, controlling for their locational setting, it is necessary to analyze the data using regression modeling frameworks (see Chapter 6).

A detailed discussion of the modeling framework is given in the Technical Appendix.

NOTES

1. This observation is the first indicator of one general expectation we had from the beginning – that the built environment activity variables would be less strongly associated with drug sales during the early part of the study period, because we would likely have inferior data for the earlier years. On the other hand, the census variables (Table 5.2), based on data collected in 1990, were expected to have stronger explanatory effects for the early part of the study period. The explanatory power of the census variables was expected to weaken over time as we moved away from 1990. The analysis of these data is discussed more fully in Chapter 6.

6. STATISTICAL ANALYSIS[1]

What Gives an Area Potential for a Drug Market?

To begin, the entire city is analyzed in order to identify the characteristics of parcels that are *not* likely to be associated with illegal drug sales as well as the characteristics of parcels that are. In other words, characteristics of the outlying wealthy areas are included in this analysis. This maximizes the variance of the analysis. Later, the "masked" city, containing only areas in which some drug-sales activity occurred, will be examined in order to determine whether different results arise when the variance is reduced by eliminating parts of the city where few, if any, drug-sales arrests occur.

Two theoretical issues are addressed in the following analyses: whether or not a parcel can contain a drug market, and if so, the size of that drug market. We expect different variables to be associated with explaining whether or not a parcel can contain a drug market than are associated with explaining the size of the market. Therefore, we are examining a two-stage process that can be analyzed by a Zero Inflated Poisson (ZIP) model. The technical aspects of this model are explained in Appendix I. This chapter reports the results of the analyses.

We begin by analyzing whether the ZIP model is the correct form for this analysis. A Vuong test value of 10.49 ($p<0.001$) confirms that the ZIP model is considerably superior to a standard Poisson regression. We prefer it to other forms of analysis, such as hurdle regression, since not only does it takes into account over-dispersion with an excess of zero values but also allows zero values to occur in the second phase where the size of the drug markets are analyzed.

We begin by looking at where illegal drug markets are likely to occur in Wilmington, Delaware. This is the first phase of the analysis in which we are attempting to identify factors associated with the existence of an illegal drug market, not its size.

Where Illegal Drug Markets Are Located

The first question is whether an area has the possibility of containing an illegal drug market. In other words, it is passing the hurdle from *cannot* to *can* have an illegal drug market. It does not analyze the size of the drug market: that is the focus of a later analysis. Table 6-1 presents the results of this analysis.[2]

An examination of Table 6-1 illustrates that four variables are statistically significant. One is the constant term for the model. The remainder can be summarized as follows:

- The Spatial Lag Term: The spatial lag term is an indication of the mean number of drug-sale arrests in the areas immediately surrounding the polygon under examination. As the number of arrests in the surrounding area increases, the chance of the local land parcel never having a drug-sale arrest diminishes.

- The Percentage of Non-White Residents: As the percentage of non-white residents in an area increases, the chance that the area will never have a drug-market arrest (i.e., will always be in the zero group) decreases.

- I-95: Being located near to an access ramp for I-95 increases the chance that an area will not have drug-market arrests.

These findings deserve some consideration. First, the spatial lag term is a measure of spatial clustering. Therefore the result from the analysis implies that if neighboring parcels contain an illegal drug market, then a given parcel is more likely to contain one (as measured in terms of drug-sales arrests). As this variable is significant, it implies the presence of positive contagion and agglomeration economies. Further evidence for this exists in the result that the size of each area is not related to the likelihood that a drug-market arrest will be made. In other words, it is not the case that larger areas will necessarily have drug-sale arrests simply because they are bigger than other areas. This suggests that clustering is taking place and facets of the urban environment other than the simple size of an area are factors. The significance of the spatial lag variable supports the notion of contagion and agglomeration with neighboring areas.

The fact that illegal drug markets tend to cluster in space in our cities is not a new finding (Weisburd and Green, 1995). It does, however, have important implications for the police and other public officials.

Table 6-1. Factors Associated with an Area Containing an Illegal Drug Market

VARIABLE	b	STD. ERR.	Z	SIGNIFICANCE
Area	-2.00e-08	1.79e-08	-1.12	0.264
Female-headed Households with Children	0.003262	0.004714	0.69	0.489
Unemployed Males	-0.01589	0.011387	-1.4	0.163
Median Income	8.55e-07	7.26e-06	0.12	0.906
Vacant Homes	-0.00417	0.008729	-0.48	0.633
Renter-occupied Units	0.002683	0.003307	0.81	0.417
Non-white Residents	**-0.01049**	**0.002771**	**-3.78**	**0.000**
Not in the same house 5 years previous	-0.018968	0.004229	-0.45	0.654
I-95	**0.338768**	**0.154307**	**2.2**	**0.028**
Major Public Transportation Interchanges	0.141274	0.392805	0.36	0.719
Check-cashing Stores	-0.05449	0.262173	-0.21	0.835
Liquor Stores	-0.01059	0.12955	-0.08	0.935
Shelters	0.12051	0.165375	0.73	0.466
Social Service Program Locations	0.16169	0.14243	1.14	0.256
Taverns	0.210624	0.135995	1.55	0.121
Spatial Lag Term	**-0.02632**	**0.008839**	**-2.98**	**0.003**
Constant	**1.082265**	**0.336751**	**3.21**	**0.001**

If positive contagion exists, it is likely to diffuse spatially over whole sections of our cities, if not addressed vigorously (for example, the South Bronx in New York City, or the Badlands of Philadelphia). If the process feeds on itself, it would be prudent for the city officials to identify its heart and take this center from the drug dealers. This is the reverse of the old practice of containment, where police would "write off" particularly crime-ridden sections of the city termed persistent high-crime areas (Schuerman and Kobrin, 1986) in order to concentrate resources on more deserving sections. This concerted effort, the reverse of containment, is the approach suggested by proponents of hot-spot policing. When practicing hot-spot policing, the police identify the worst areas where crime is spatially concentrated and focus their attention and resources on these areas. But what are these areas like beyond being clustered in space? We begin by examining the factors generally associated with social disorganization and demographic factors related to demand for illegal drugs.

We find mixed results when variables commonly associated with social disorganization and social efficacy are examined (Table 6-1). Many features commonly associated with concepts of social disorganization are not statistically significant, including the percentage of female-headed households with children, the percentage of unemployed males, or measures of population turnover (those living in the same house as they did five years ago) or income. Also, aspects of the housing market (percentage of homes unoccupied or occupied by renters) were not significant. However, one variable was clearly noticeable. The proportion of residents who were non-white was more significant (statistically) than any other variable.

As the proportion of non-white residents increases, the likelihood that the area will have drug-sales arrests increases. This is a highly disturbing finding. We must ask why minority neighborhoods are particularly vulnerable to the establishment of illegal drug markets. If illegal drug markets locate in vulnerable neighborhoods, why are these neighborhoods so vulnerable in the first place? There are several theoretical explanations for this relationship. Perhaps the most often heard is Anderson's (1999) "code of the streets," in which black residents (especially young males) feel they have to handle their own problems rather than rely on the police. If the police are not called upon to confront drug problems in a neighborhood, one of the most important tools available to the community is lost. One should never attempt to beat another at his or her own game. The business or "game" of drug dealers is to market drugs. Dealers have much more time and know-how than the neighbors. Only the police can level the playing field. But why would African-American neighbors not rely on the police to solve their problems?

One idea is that the "code of the streets" has an extensive history beyond the inner city. Nisbett and Cohen (1996) point out that blacks living in the rural south never could rely on the police to address their problems of injustice. After the Civil War, many whites also did not rely on the police and, instead, formed vigilante groups such as the Ku Klux Klan. The reasoning here is that if you wish to perpetuate an irrational system that regards some humans are inferior to others based on their race, the only way to enforce this is through violence, since reasoning does not hold up to scrutiny. Therefore, slave owners used violence to control slaves and vigilante groups used violence to control blacks following emancipation.

Under this system, blacks did not have consistent access to the police to handle their problems, especially if a black person was accusing a white person of an injustice. If they could not rely on the police, the only alternative for African Americans was to handle the matter personally. This, in turn, left two alternatives: the first was to do nothing and leave oneself vulnerable to repeat victimization. The second was to use violence to defend oneself and to send a clear message that repeat victimization would come with a price to the perpetrator. One can make the argument that the "code of the streets" in the inner city is nothing more than a continuation of the code of honor and survival in the rural south where earlier generations of blacks lived and were socialized (Baumer, 2002).

Anderson (1999) develops the idea of a street code much more fully. He implies an inverse effect of neighborhood disadvantage on victim crime reporting. This is especially the case among victims who live in extremely disadvantaged neighborhoods who are young, black and males. Anderson (1999:34) identifies three mechanisms that might inhibit crime reporting by these types of victims:

(1) High rates of poverty and joblessness instill in young males a " . . . sense of alienation from mainstream society and its institutions . . . a profound lack of faith in the police and judicial

system – and in others who would champion one's personal security."

(2) As an adaptation to their alienation, many disadvantaged young black males embrace the "code of the street," that prescribes the proper way to respond to interpersonal violence.

(3) Blocked access to legitimate economic opportunities and associated feelings of hopelessness and alienation push some disadvantaged young black males to become involved in the underground economy, including drug dealing.

Anderson (1999) therefore defines an inverse relationship between neighborhood disadvantage, drug dealing and police notification. According to this reasoning, residents of disadvantaged neighborhoods are not likely to rely on the police to solve their problems. Anderson (1999:321) explains this reasoning: "Residents sometimes fail to call the police because they believe that the police are unlikely to come or, if they do come, may even harass the very people who called them." Rather than rely on the police to solve their problems, the "code" expects them to take personal responsibility for one's safety. It defines as weak and cowardly those who rely on the police. In fact, those who call the police may face reprisals. This has been the case for some neighbors who were beaten by drug dealers for calling the police (Lacayo, 1989; Graham and Ott, 2004).

There is no general agreement that socially disorganized disadvantaged residents of a neighborhood are less likely to call the police to solve their problems. Gottfredson and Hindelang (1979) and Laub (1980) argue that in areas with ineffective informal social controls, there may be more of a need for and reliance on formal social control mechanisms such as the police to handle perceived injustices such as interpersonal disputes and to reduce future vulnerability to criminal victimization. Furthermore, low-income black inner-city residents do not necessarily have thin social networks (Morenoff et al., 2001). They may be highly connected, but may or may not rely on the police to solve their interpersonal disputes.

One of the most comprehensive studies of race, social disadvantage and notification of the police was completed by Baumer (2002), using data from the Area-Identified National Crime Victimization Survey. In contrast to Anderson's (1999) ethnographic research findings, Baumer (2002) discovered that residents of disadvantaged neighborhoods are not uniformly less likely to notify the police when they are victimized.

In fact, the most affluent are just as unlikely to call the police as the least affluent. Baumer (2002:605-606) sums his findings as follows:

> ... the influence of neighborhood disadvantage on police notification does not appear to be particularly salient for ... central cities, young persons, blacks, or males ... if a distinctive "code" exists in disadvantaged central-city neighborhoods, it does not translate into significantly lower rates of police notification. It may be that the "code" to which Anderson (1999) refers is not limited to central cities ... but is much more geographically and demographically dispersed than his research implies.

Using Wilmington data, we discovered that police calls-for-service statistics closely mirrored the arrest data. There was no evidence at the city level of analysis that neighborhoods that experienced the most drug-sales arrests were the least likely to call the police for assistance (see Figure 6-1 for a comparison). Furthermore, an examination of the data did not identify any neighborhood whose residents were refusing to call the police on a consistent basis, at least in respect of drug-related calls. Going further, there was no apparent evidence that residents of predominantly black communities were calling the police at a reduced rate compared to other areas. In fact, calls to the police seem to cluster spatially in the inner-city areas where black residents tended to reside.

This brings us to the second group of factors, those related to the accessibility of an area. Of the two factors analyzed, one was statistically significant. Only the buffers around I-95 exits were statistically significant, but not in the direction theoretically proposed. Public transportation hubs such as the Amtrak station and bus stations were not statistically significant. This is not an unexpected result since in our examination of the location quotients, there was a lack of stability over time.

Proximity to an access ramp of I-95 appears to increase the likelihood that an area will not have any drug-sales arrests. As will be shown in Table 6-2 however, accessibility to I-95 *increases* the number of drug-sales arrests *if* a drug market exists. Although on first reading this may appear contradictory, we can hypothesize the following in regard to this finding. Not all exit ramps are the same. Although we know from the location quotient analysis that, across the city, there is a clustering of drug-sales arrests 1,200 to 1,600 feet from an exit ramp (see Technical Appendix), this does not hold for every exit ramp. The number of locations approximately three blocks from an exit ramp in Wilmington

Figure 6-1. Density of Drug-related Calls for Service and Arrests, 1989-1991

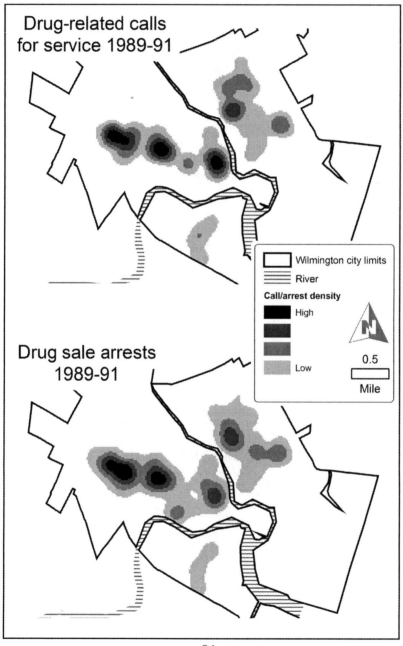

Table 6-2.   Factors Associated with the Size of an Illegal Drug Market

VARIABLE	b	STD. ERR.	Z	SIGNIFICANCE
Area	7.98E-09	2.22E-09	3.59	0.000
Female-headed Households with Children	**0.007283**	**0.001092**	**6.67**	**0.000**
Unemployed Males	-0.00373	0.002161	-1.73	0.084
Median Income	3.82E-06	2.06E-06	1.86	0.063
Vacant Homes	**0.023534**	**0.00194**	**12.13**	**0.000**
Renter-occupied Units	**-0.01168**	**0.000949**	**-12.3**	**0.000**
Non-white Residents	**0.021957**	**0.000814**	**26.98**	**0.000**
Not in the same house 5 years previous	0.000429	0.001175	0.37	0.715
I-95	**0.357078**	**0.031727**	**11.25**	**0.000**
Major Public Transportation Interchanges	0.069235	0.094737	0.73	0.465
Check-cashing Stores	**0.231319**	**0.063936**	**3.62**	**0.000**
Liquor Stores	**0.096299**	**0.026089**	**3.69**	**0.000**
Shelters	**0.369729**	**0.031882**	**11.6**	**0.000**
Social Service Program Locations	**-0.12605**	**0.029601**	**-4.26**	**0.000**
Taverns	**-0.06941**	**0.033031**	**-2.1**	**0.036**
Spatial Lag Term	**0.011969**	**0.000578**	**20.71**	**0.000**
Constant	**0.724153**	**0.131296**	**5.52**	**0.000**

without drug-sales arrests are sufficiently numerous to cause the statistically significant finding shown in Table 6-1. Bear in mind, though, that Table 6-2 shows that if one does develop, the proximity to the exit ramp works in conjunction with other factors to make the area attractive to drug dealers. In this respect, some I-95 exits follow theoretical expectations that lead us to expect that major transportation arteries funneling regional residents into the city are likely to contain illegal drug markets (in at least some locations). Others do not.

That the rail and bus stations were not significantly related to illegal drug sales was unexpected. Perhaps these modes of transportation are more likely to be used by occasional passengers, and a person getting off the train or bus may be more concerned with finding her or his destination than with buying illegal drugs in a strange place.

Finally, many of the built facilities that are used on a routine basis by potential drug users were not statistically related to the existence of illegal drug markets. Contrary to our theoretical expectations, taverns were not significantly related to the existence of illegal drug markets. It seems that taverns do not have the same relationship to illegal drug markets in Wilmington as they do to crime in other settings (Roncek and Bell, 1981; Roncek and Pravatiner, 1989). Social service centers (such as drug treatment centers) were not statistically related to illegal drug markets. Perhaps social service centers that treat drug addicts also control the area surrounding their facilities more than was anticipated. In other words, the employees of these centers may act as "place managers" for the immediate locale.

Check cashing stores, liquor stores and homeless shelters were not significant in this initial part of the analysis. In other words, these locations had high location quotients because they were located near other explanatory variables. Once the variance was explained by the other explanatory variables, these facilities were not significantly related to the development of drug-market areas.

In summary, important variables from each category were significantly related to the establishment of an illegal drug market. The most important variables were the percentage of non-white residents and proximity to I-95 exits. Also very important was the spatial lag term that suggests that illegal drug markets tend to cluster in space. This finding lends support to the notion of positive contagion, where illegal drug sales creep outward from a center much like a wine stain on a white table cloth. Once illegal drug sales become established in an area, surrounding areas are more likely to contain illegal drug markets as well.

It will be interesting to see if these variables also influence the size of a drug market. For example, if a site becomes known as a place to sell illegal drugs, it might become large through agglomeration economies, but surrounding sites may remain small or non-existent if the attraction to the large site is great. In other words, we would not expect large illegal drug markets to cluster spatially near each other. As explained in "central place theory" of geography, there will be many more small market places than large ones, and the small places will be located closer to each other than large centers (Norris et al., 1982).

We must keep in mind that the variables analyzed above are related to the establishment of illegal drug sales, not to the size of the sales operation. In the next section, the analysis determines which variables are related to the size of the sales operation in each parcel.

Factors Associated with the Size of a Drug Market

The second phase of the ZIP model determines what factors are statistically associated with the size of an illegal drug market, given that the area is susceptible. This stage in the process estimates the model parameters for the group of locations that the first part predicted as capable of sustaining a local drug market (based on arrest statistics). In other words, in this part of the study, we consider what factors influence the number of arrests if an area is vulnerable to drug-market arrests. Table 6-2 presents the results of this analysis (factors that are statistically significant are shown in bold print). Many of the findings are as we would expect theoretically.

Other than the model constant (which is significant as we would expect), we also find that the area and spatial lag term are significant. This is not surprising. We would expect that, all other things being equal, the larger a polygon the more likely that it would have a greater number of drug market arrests. In the first part of the model the spatial lag term was a predictor of membership of the "could not have drug market arrests" group. As the number of drug-market arrests in the neighboring areas increased, then the likelihood of the area under examination not having arrests declined. As we find in this part of the study, if neighboring areas have arrests, the land parcel under examination will have more arrests. In other words, as the number of arrests in the surrounding area increases, so does the local arrest level. This provides support for the argument that large drug markets are likely to be located near each other. In other words, the larger the market, the more likely it is to have another large market in a neighboring parcel. This implies that clustering of drug market areas is a significant problem for Wilmington. It also implies that contrary to the ideas of "central place theory" in geography, large illegal drug markets are not scattered broadly throughout the city, but rather are clustered in space. In other words, rather than the negative contagion of central place theory, there seems to be positive contagion of agglomeration economies that suggests that as an area becomes known as a place to purchase illegal drugs, surrounding areas are more likely to contain a large drug market to siphon off some of the excess business beyond the threshold level required to keep the drug dealers in business.

The second group of variables is commonly associated with the concepts of social disorganization. Neither the percentage of unemployed males in an area nor the median household income is significant at the level determined for this study. The rate of population turnover is also not significant (the number of people who resided in the same house five years previously).

Two variables do follow our expectations from social disorganization theory. One focuses on the family, and the other on the neighborhood. Concerning the family: when the proportion of female-headed households with children under five increases, the number of drug-market arrests in areas that are capable of containing drug markets increases. From the neighborhood perspective, when the percentage of vacant homes increases in an area, the number of drug-market arrests increases (assuming the area contains the potential for an illegal drug market). This latter finding is not surprising from a social disorganization perspective: abandoned houses do not translate into a socially organized neighborhood. However, from an economic perspective, it is somewhat surprising since a neighborhood with a lot of abandoned houses is not likely to contain as many potential customers as one that has occupied homes.

The b value of the female-headed households is relatively small, yet the finding follows closely the ethnographic work of Dunlap and his colleagues in New York City (Dunlap, 1992; Johnson et al., 2000). These authors note that female-headed households often have a transient male passing through who may have drug problems, and that the partners are much less likely to have a committed relationship than other households. Furthermore, without a partner the female head of household will have much more difficulty focusing beyond her family toward community concerns than if the family is intact with two adults. In any case, areas that have more single-female households with children under five and have the potential for drug markets also are more likely to have a larger drug market.

As Table 6-2 shows, the number of renter-occupied units is significant, but not in the direction expected theoretically. At least in Wilmington, as the number of renter occupied units increases, the potential size of a drug market decreases. Concerning renter-occupied units, Lersch (2004:43) sums up the theoretical expectations nicely:

> It should not be inferred that people who rent are the cause of criminal activity. Most people will rent a home or apartment at some point in our lives. However, if a person is renting their home, their living arrangement is by definition temporary in nature. Generally speaking, renters do not share the same stake in the community as homeowners do. Renters come and go at the end of their lease, while homeowners tend to reside in neighborhoods for a longer period of time and therefore tend to identify with their community to a greater extent. . . . Neighborhoods with high numbers of rental units tend to be less stable and socially organized than areas with fewer rental units.

However, in the case of Wilmington, there is a very high proportion of renter-occupied units in the city. Perhaps many of these renters consider their units to be as permanent as do homeowners. This would seem to be the case for rent-controlled units in New York City. Many of us have known persons who have rented their entire lives. We may be thinking ethnocentrically if we consider all persons who rent as living in temporary housing. Clearly, this factor requires further investigation in other settings.

The final factor related to social disorganization is the percentage of non-white residents in an area. Unfortunately the findings are clear. If an area does have the potential to contain a drug market, then the percentage of non-white residents in the area is a significant factor in determining the size of the drug market.

As explained in the first part of the ZIP model, the percentage of non-white residents is related to the potential to establish drug markets. A follow-on from this finding is that there is also a relationship between the percentage of non-white residents and the size of the drug market. In other words, the higher the proportion of non-white residents living in an area, the larger the illegal drug market is likely to be.

The final group of factors relates to the accessibility of an area. The majority of factors follow our expectations in regard to the size of a drug market. Although the first part of the ZIP model indicated that being within three to four blocks of an exit ramp for I-95 increased the chance that an area would never have a drug market, the second part of the analysis shows that if a drug market does exist, then proximity to I-95 is a factor in determining the size of the market. Where drug arrests are made, being within three blocks of I-95 increases the number of arrests. In other words, locations three blocks from exits of this limited-access highway were positively associated with the size of illegal drug markets. It is interesting that major roads did not have a location quotient above 2, and thus were not included in our analysis. The buffer of 400 feet around major roads took up over 50% of the study area. Perhaps this is too generous a definition of major roads. The fact that some I-95 exits were associated with greater illegal drug-sales arrests leads us to believe that only the most important highways, not highways in general, are associated with illegal drug sales in Wilmington, and not all exits from I-95, but only exits in certain areas contain illegal drug markets. This finding is similar to that of Eck (1997), who illustrated that only major highways' intersections within certain parts of the city (lower socioeconomic areas) attract illegal drug dealers. Since these areas are expected to serve regional customers funneled into the city, they are likely to house large open-air markets that are easy for police to locate, but are profitable enough that arrests do not seem to curb their activities.

This is not a particularly surprising finding if one ponders the theoretical issues. In fact, this statistical result supports Eck's (1994) findings that drug markets tend to cluster around major highways. Perhaps in the present analysis we were too generous in our definition of a major highway (the buffers of 400 feet covered over half the study area). When we consider really major highways (such as limited access I-95), exits seem to be associated with the size of illegal drug markets measured in terms of illegal drug-sales arrests.

This may also explain why the major public transport interchanges were not significant. Local regional customers wishing to purchase drugs in the Wilmington area may find it easier to purchase illegal drugs from their car window within a few blocks of certain I-95 exits rather than being seen around the bus or train stations. There is also the possibility that local law enforcement or other place managers could be providing place management around the public transport intersections.

Liquor stores and check-cashing stores tended to influence the size of illegal drug markets on the same block. Both of these findings follow our theoretical expectations. Many drug users are poly-drug users who like to drink alcohol at the same time as they are consuming a controlled substance. Check-cashing stores tend to be used by those who need ready cash but who do not have access to a regular bank.

The facility with the highest z score was a homeless shelter. This implies that drug markets located two blocks from homeless shelters have the capacity to grow. This supports our theoretical reasoning that a significant proportion of homeless individuals are likely to use controlled substances, and therefore illegal drug dealers have an incentive to locate as close to a homeless shelter as is prudent. In Wilmington, this tends to be about a block away.

On the other hand, homeless shelters may locate near their clients, who stay in areas that have a high potential for drug-sales arrests for other reasons. However, when many of these other factors are taken into account statistically, homeless shelters remained a significant factor related to the size of illegal drug-sales arrests. Still, it may be that the drug-sales arrests would be high in these locations whether or not a homeless shelter is located nearby. Our analysis does not allow us to say that a homeless shelter causes drug-sales arrests to cluster in the surrounding area. It only allows us to say that drug-sales arrests do cluster spatially where homeless shelters are located. There is an important difference here that will be discussed more fully in the following chapters of this book.

There are two surprising outcomes from the analysis. Both the locations of social service programs and the locations of taverns are statistically significant, but their coefficients do not run in the direction expected. There are no theoretical explanations for these two findings. Neither follows our expectations from social disorganization theory.

Although the social service program locations are significant, the coefficient (b) is negative. This means that in areas where drug markets may exist, the program exerts a dampening influence on the size of the market. Again, a possible explanation for this is the impact of place managers at certain locations. As we suggested in Chapter 5, immediately around a social service center drug dealers would have difficulty operating because of the extra security and scrutiny. The location quotient analysis in the preceding chapter suggested a peak in the buffer from 400 to 800 feet, however this examined the impact of the buffer analysis without the inclusion of other factors. The result from the ZIP model suggests that when other factors are accounted for, the presence of a social service program center has a dampening effect on the size of the drug market.

The most surprising finding is the negative impact of taverns in the Wilmington area. In other words, the presence of a tavern in a parcel meant that a smaller rather than a larger illegal drug market was likely. The coefficient value and the z score suggest that this is not a strong influence, but it is nevertheless significant statistically. This is a very interesting result. It may be due to nuisance laws that allow a liquor license to be revoked if tavern owners allow illegal drug sales in their establishments. Tavern owners may act as effective place managers keeping illegal drug sales under control. Unlike liquor stores where a bottle is purchased and consumed off the premises, a tavern is a place where liquor is consumed within the establishment. Therefore, it is not likely to provide enough customers for drug dealers in the surrounding areas since most of the patrons' time is spent within the establishment. Therefore, taverns are spatially associated with small drug markets but negatively associated with large drug markets. It could be that a large drug market is considered bad for business and could drive tavern users away from the location, whereas a small operation is able to operate "under the radar" of the tavern owner without having a detrimental impact on the business of the bar. Perhaps these small, local operations actually work within the bar. This could be the type of neighborhood market proposed by Eck (1994) as a result of his study in San Diego (see Chapter 4 for the details of this study). If the market in the area of a tavern is a neighborhood one, it is, by definition, local and closed. By limiting drug sales to the local community, the market will be unable to significantly expand and will therefore remain relatively small. This may explain why our study found that taverns act as a limiting factor in the size of a drug market, in effect acting as a dampening influence.

It must be borne in mind that these results are aggregated for the whole city, and as will be seen in the next chapter, some taverns have few arrests if any, whereas others attract considerable police attention. The influence of local context is therefore important, and suggests the value of a problem-oriented approach, as discussed in Chapter 3.

Analysis of the Masked City

To be complete, we include an analysis of the masked city, which excluded relatively wealthy outlying areas where drug-sales arrests are not likely to take place. Tables 6-3 and 6-4 present these results. What is notable about these two tables is their similarity to the tables in which

Table 6-3. Masked City: Factors Associated with an Area Containing an Illegal Drug Market

VARIABLE	b	STD. ERR.	Z	SIGNIFICANCE
Area	-2.32e-08	2.08e-08	-1.12	0.265
Female-headed Households with Children	.0021829	.0047867	0.46	0.648
Unemployed Males	-.0139461	.0115954	-1.20	0.229
Median Income	-3.61e-06	8.01e-06	-0.45	0.652
Vacant Homes	-.0028891	.0089228	-0.32	0.746
Renter-occupied Units	.0038703	.0035632	1.09	0.277
Non-white Residents	**-.0079996**	**.002864**	**-2.79**	**0.005**
In the same house 5 years previous	.0010387	.0045272	0.23	0.819
I-95	**.4524311**	**.1587835**	**2.85**	**0.004**
Major Public Transportation Interchanges	.3498079	.3947182	0.89	0.375
Check Cashing Stores	.015602	.2661311	0.06	0.953
Liquor Stores	-.043282	.1337066	-0.32	0.746
Shelters	.1891123	.1686137	1.12	0.262
Social Service Program Locations	.1764511	.1466926	1.20	0.229
Taverns	**.3356667**	**.1400619**	**2.40**	**0.017**
Spatial Lag Term	**-.0262752**	**.0089832**	**-2.92**	**0.003**
Constant	**1.065035**	**.4167721**	**2.56**	**0.011**

Table 6-4. Masked City: Factors Associated with the Size of an Illegal Drug Market

VARIABLE	b	STD. ERR.	Z	SIGNIFICANCE
Area	**7.14e-09**	**2.26e-09**	**3.15**	**0.002**
Female-headed Households with Children	**.0073973**	**.0011085**	**6.67**	**0.000**
Unemployed Males	-.0038349	.0021768	-1.76	0.078
Median Income	4.00e-06	2.09e-06	1.91	0.056
Vacant Homes	**.0226036**	**.0019606**	**11.53**	**0.000**
Renter-occupied Units	**-.011781**	**.0009593**	**-12.28**	**0.000**
Non-white Residents	**.0215693**	**.0008111**	**26.59**	**0.000**
In the same house 5 years previous	.0004655	.0011948	0.39	0.697
I-95	**.3497757**	**.0318853**	**10.97**	**0.000**
Major Public Transportation interchanges	.0951754	.0950419	1.00	0.317
Check-cashing Stores	**.2354375**	**.064264**	**3.66**	**0.000**
Liquor Stores	**.1035715**	**.0262455**	**3.95**	**0.000**
Shelters	**.3741217**	**.0325325**	**11.50**	**0.000**
Social Service Program Locations	**-.113636**	**.0297322**	**-3.82**	**0.000**
Taverns	**-.0585879**	**.0334766**	**-1.75**	**0.080**
Spatial Lag Term	**.0119765**	**.0005843**	**20.50**	**0.000**
Constant	**.8332764**	**.1365549**	**6.10**	**0.000**

the entire city was presented. The only notable difference is that, when wealthy outlying areas with their associated taverns were masked from the analysis, taverns became a significant explanatory variable concerning the potential for establishment of drug markets. Within the masked city area, the presence of a tavern increases the probability that a parcel will not have any drug arrests. In other words, taverns become important within their context. It may be that the neighborhood markets discussed in the preceding section are more congregated in the wealthy neighborhoods, whereas some of the city-center bars are conscious of attracting police attention, and some locations in the city actively work (either with local residents, police or even by themselves as place managers) to dissuade drug markets from establishing in the locale. We will discuss this further in the following chapters.

SUMMARY

The statistical analysis conducted here discovered that many of the expected causes of drug markets were found to be statistically significant in the initial (ZIP) analysis of drug market viability. The ZIP model works in two ways. In our example, the first method examines what factors might influence whether an area has the potential to house a drug market. The second method explores the range of factors that might influence the size of a market.

As the spatial lag term illustrated, the existence of drug arrests in surrounding areas predicted the likelihood that an area had the potential to have drug arrests, as did the proportion of non-white residents in a parcel. Interestingly, proximity to I-95 worked as a slight inhibitor to the potential for drug market evolvement.

As expected, most of the features that showed clustering of drug arrests in their vicinity from the location quotient analysis were significant predictors of the size of a drug market in the second part of the ZIP model analysis. Exceptions were the location of social service centers and taverns, and the percentage of renter-occupied units, all factors negatively associated with the size of an illegal drug market. Median income, the unemployment rate among males, the proportion of residents who live in the same house as they did five years ago, and the presence of bus and train stations were not statistically significantly related to the size of illegal drug markets in areas of Wilmington that were potentially susceptible to drug markets.

Interestingly, the spatial lag variable was consistently significant throughout. If the surrounding area had drug markets, then it was more likely that a drug market would exist. Furthermore, if a drug market did exist, then increased number of arrests in surrounding areas were related to higher numbers of arrests in the land parcel. These results, on the whole, tell us what we expected: that agglomeration economies are dominant in street drug markets, and that many of the factors associated with susceptibility, activity, and accessibility correlate with the potential to increase the size of a drug market.

Finally, the most productive markets (in terms of numbers of drug-sales arrests, and based on the z score values) were likely to be found in the vicinity of homeless shelters, and in areas where greater percentages of non-white residents lived. These are very intriguing findings that are discussed more fully in the next chapter.

NOTES

1. This and the preceding chapter describe the statistical analyses that were conducted in Wilmington to explore the distribution of drug arrests in the city. By necessity, the text gets a bit technical in some places. This is required because we think our approach is innovative as well as statistically robust. By explaining the techniques and findings in detail, we hope to provide other researchers with the opportunity to replicate this type of study and learn about additional cities. However, we also recognize that some readers may not wish to delve deeply into the statistics. For non-technical readers, a summary of the significant findings can be found in Chapter 7.

2. Table 6-1 reports the ZIP values that predict an area will not contain illegal drug markets as measured by drug sales arrests. The parameters of the variables indicate the value of using that particular variable to predict there will be no drug sales arrests in the associated area. The interpretation of the signs of the parameters may seem counterintuitive to the reader. Generally we interpret positive signs to mean moving forward such as crossing the hurdle from no drug sales arrests to some drug sales arrests. In the first phase of the ZIP model however, increasing positive values mean that there is greater likelihood that the hurdle from no to some drug sales arrests will not be crossed. In other words, a significant positive value of the

coefficient (b value) indicates that an increase in that variable will increase the probability that an area will not have any illegal drug sales arrests. Conversely, significant negative values predict that an area will have illegal drug sales arrests.

7. INTERPRETATION OF THE FINDINGS

Before proceeding to discuss the findings, it may be useful to recap with a short summary of the key findings of the study to this point.

Spatial Analysis

- The location-allocation model proved successful in predicting likely areas of drug markets (at the census tract level).

- From location quotients we know that drug arrests cluster around many of the expected urban features that might encourage drug sales, such as homeless shelters and check cashing stores. The optimum distance for drug-sale arrests differs for the various types of feature.

ZIP Model: The Potential to Establish a Market

- The Zero Inflated Poisson (ZIP) model of the whole city found statistically significant levels of spatial lag. This suggests if a neighboring parcel contains an illegal drug market, then a given parcel is more likely to contain one (as measured in terms of drug-sales arrests). This finding implies positive contagion.

- We found mixed results when variables commonly associated with social disorganization and social efficacy were examined. Most factors were not statistically significant.

- The proportion of non-white residents was positively related to drug-sale arrests and had the highest (absolute) z score. This raises the question as to why minority neighborhoods are particularly vulnerable to the establishment of illegal drug markets.

- The buffers around I-95 exits were statistically significant, but not in the expected direction. Being within three to four blocks of an exit ramp inhibited the development of drug markets. However as the next section points out, the impact of an exit ramp is different once a drug market is established.

- Public transportation hubs such as the Amtrak station and bus stations were not statistically significant.

- Contrary to our theoretical expectations, taverns were not significantly related to the establishment of illegal drug markets for the whole city. In the central part of the city (the masked area), their presence hindered the establishment of an illegal drug market.

ZIP Model: The Potential to Inflate the Size of an Existing Market

- The ZIP model found statistically significant levels of spatial lag for the size of a drug market. This means that local drug markets will tend to increase as the size of the drug markets in neighboring areas increases. This provides strong evidence for contagion and agglomeration economies.

- Public transportation hubs such as the Amtrak station and bus stations were not statistically significant.

- Contrary to expectations, both social service program locations and taverns effected a dampening influence on the size of existing drug markets. This suggests that a degree of place management is taking place around these locations.

- Check-cashing stores, liquor stores and homeless shelters were all positively associated with increases in the size of drug markets. Homeless shelters demonstrated the largest z score, suggesting that homeless shelters exert a strong influence on drug market size.

- As the percentage of vacant homes in an area increased, the size of local drug markets was likely to increase.

- The percentage of non-white residents was related to the size of the drug markets measured in terms of illegal drug-sales arrests. In other words, the greater the percentage of non-white residents in a parcel, the larger the illegal drug market was likely to be.

- In the masked city analysis, taverns became a significant, inverse explanatory variable concerning the development of drug markets when wealthy outlying areas with their associated taverns were masked from the analysis. In other words, taverns only become influential as inhibitors of drug sales in locations within the city center.

WHAT DOES THIS ALL MEAN?

Factors from each category explained whether or not a drug market would exist in a parcel. Many fewer factors explained the initial development of drug markets. In fact, only two factors were positively associated with the development of drug markets in the parcels: the percentage of non-white residents living in the area, and the mean number of drug arrests in the surrounding area up to a block and a half. When we examine each category of variables, beginning with susceptibility factors associated with whether a drug market exists, we identify some interesting findings.

Susceptibility

The primary element of susceptibility to street drug markets is the racial makeup of the population. Areas of the inner city where minorities dominate in demographic terms are areas where drug-sales arrests are most likely to take place. Income (or lack of it) was not an important statistical factor in any of our ZIP models. This is a very intriguing finding.

  We looked into this issue further, as we were puzzled that income was not more strongly related to drug-sales arrests than the percentage of non-white residents. Figure 7-1 maps the overlay of income and arrest points for one example year (1989), and the reason for the relative lack of strength of the income-drug sales relationship becomes clear. A few drug-sales arrests are concentrated on the outside edges of the lowest income areas. But in general, drug-sales arrests tend to concentrate not in the center of the lowest-income areas (perhaps because these areas are too poor to support expensive drug habits), but in the next highest-income areas. And, as expected, the drug-sales arrests tend to be absent in the highest-income areas. Threshold conditions must be met if illegal drugs are to be sold to local residents. There are two

Figure 7-1.   Median Household Income and Drug-Sales Arrests: 1989
(income data from the 1990 census)

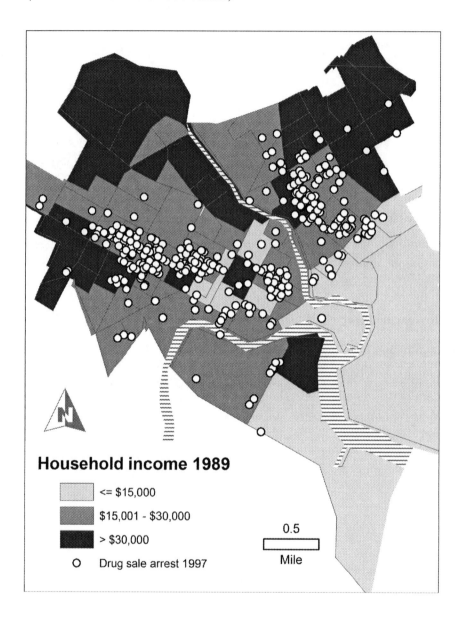

Household income 1989

<= $15,000

$15,001 - $30,000

> $30,000

O   Drug sale arrest 1997

0.5

Mile

components to threshold conditions, disposable income of the residents of a community, and the number of potential drug users in the community. Moore and Kleiman (1997:231) note the importance of income to support an illegal drug market:

> . . . in a review of the spatial distribution of drug dealing across a city. In some areas, drug dealers cannot gain a foothold. There are too few users to make dealing profitable. . . . This finding, we believe, is important in understanding the nature of local illegal drug markets.

Another critical question is whether the built environment has any influence on the size of illegal drug markets. After all, there was clear evidence of significantly high location quotients around the selected built environment feature types. As expected, many of the features associated with destinations of potential drug users were positively associated with the size of an illegal drug market, once it had been established. This was not a surprising finding since most were associated with the existence of a drug market, though there were a couple of accessibility features which did not behave as expected, as will be explained later in the chapter. One susceptibility factor also behaved in an unexpected manner: the percentage of renter-occupied units. The next section examines this finding in more detail.

The Influence of Rental Markets and Minority Areas

The renter-occupied variable seems somewhat of a paradox. Contrary to expectations, the percentage of renter-occupied units was significantly and inversely related to the size of drug markets in a parcel. There is no clear explanation for this relationship. Speculation could lead one to believe that renter-occupied units in the inner city may be more stable than currently believed (Lersch, 2004). This might mean more guardianship of the surrounding sidewalk, rather than less, since the housing units may not be so "hardened" with the locks, gratings and alarms that single-family homes in the same areas contain. When families make themselves safe through the use of alarms and gratings in the inner city, they are not as likely to rely on social means of crime control. Their attitude may be, "I am safe in my home, let the police handle whatever happens on the street or sidewalk." On the other hand, renters without this personal security may rely more on social means of crime control and/or include the police in their efforts. Renters also are more likely to be densely populated in their neighborhoods, with more housing units per block than if the block contained single-family homes. This translates into more use of the neighborhood than would be the case in single-family areas. In Wilmington, renter-occupied units constitute one-third of the housing units in the city. Perhaps due to the relatively high proportion of rental dwellings, this type of housing did not equate to social disorganization or any other theoretical variable that would encourage illegal drug sales. Clearly, further research is required to disentangle this issue.

What is clear is that minority-dominated neighborhoods are highly and consistently related to drug-sales arrests. In this instance, there is a great deal of theory and some prior research on which to base these findings. First, this analysis appears to point to an old critique of urban planning – that the planning systems operate so that the most noxious facilities end up being located in vulnerable neighborhoods: minority-dominated areas that are often unable to combat or mobilize against undesirable private or public facilities in their backyards (Smith, 1986). This critique suggests that noxious facilities, such as drug markets, locate where they do because the populations are vulnerable or susceptible; hence the susceptibility of the population is the key factor, the type of facility is not.

The Importance of Local Context

This leads to the second explanation, that all facilities of a class (say liquor stores or taverns) are not equally noxious. They are noxious within their local contexts. In other words, the effects of liquor stores or taverns are not homogenous across space (that was a presumption underlying the modeling approach), but are geographically contextual. There are "good" taverns and "bad" taverns. One will rarely find the latter in high-income white neighborhoods; this does not mean that all taverns in low-income minority-dominated areas are "bad," but the likelihood of the tavern and the area surrounding such establishments being bad and then tolerated in such neighborhoods is higher.

You may remember, from Chapter 6, that taverns and liquor stores were not associated with the potential to develop a drug market, except in the central part of the city where the presence of a tavern on the block decreased the likelihood of a drug market existing. If a drug market did exist, then a liquor store on the corner had the effect of *increasing* drug-sales arrests, while a tavern on the corner *decreased* the size of the drug market.

Figures 7-2 and 7-3 show the distribution of liquor stores and taverns in the study area, and the number of drug-sale arrests in their vicinities in 1997. The distribution of the stores and taverns in the figures is clearly clustered (for taverns more so than liquor stores) in the low- to middle-income minority-dominated areas, and close to I-95 exits. Which came first, and which of these factors were most important? With the exception of I-95 exits, the models suggest that the susceptible population came first, and that the built environment and drug arrests were both consequences of the susceptibility of the population.

Figures 7-2 and 7-3 reinforce the findings from the whole study. The overall impact, when aggregated to the whole city, is that drug markets cluster around taverns and liquor stores. This is evidenced by the location quotient analysis. However hidden within this city-wide analysis is the reality that there are good and bad taverns, and good and bad liquor stores. Taverns in particular, seem to exhibit a positive influence on the local block, at least in most of the inner city of Wilmington. As Figure 7-3 shows, this positive influence does not apply to the whole city. One neighborhood is particularly plagued by drug markets, markets which appear to have reached a tipping point and are demonstrating an agglomeration economy. As we explain later in this chapter, broad-brush solutions applied city-wide may not be the solution: local context and place is the key. Of course, the local community makes up much of the local context, and in certain areas (see figures 7-2 and 7-3) the community is vulnerable to the presence of drug markets.

Could it be that some communities are susceptible because they do not use the police or other public resources to assist them in countering the forces of illegal drug dealers? One way to determine whether this is true is to examine the spatial pattern of calls for police service, as noted previously. Using Wilmington data, we discovered that calls-for-service data closely mirrored the arrest data. There was no evidence at the city level of analysis that any neighborhood's residents were consistently unwilling to call the police. In fact, the calls for service to the police mirrored very closely the spatial pattern of drug-sales arrests (see Figure 6-1). Yet an examination of the yearly arrests by census tract, discussed in Chapter 4, demonstrated a relatively consistent pattern year to year. In other words, the police are making arrests, but the problems

Figure 7-2. Arrests within 400 Feet of Liquor Stores: 1997

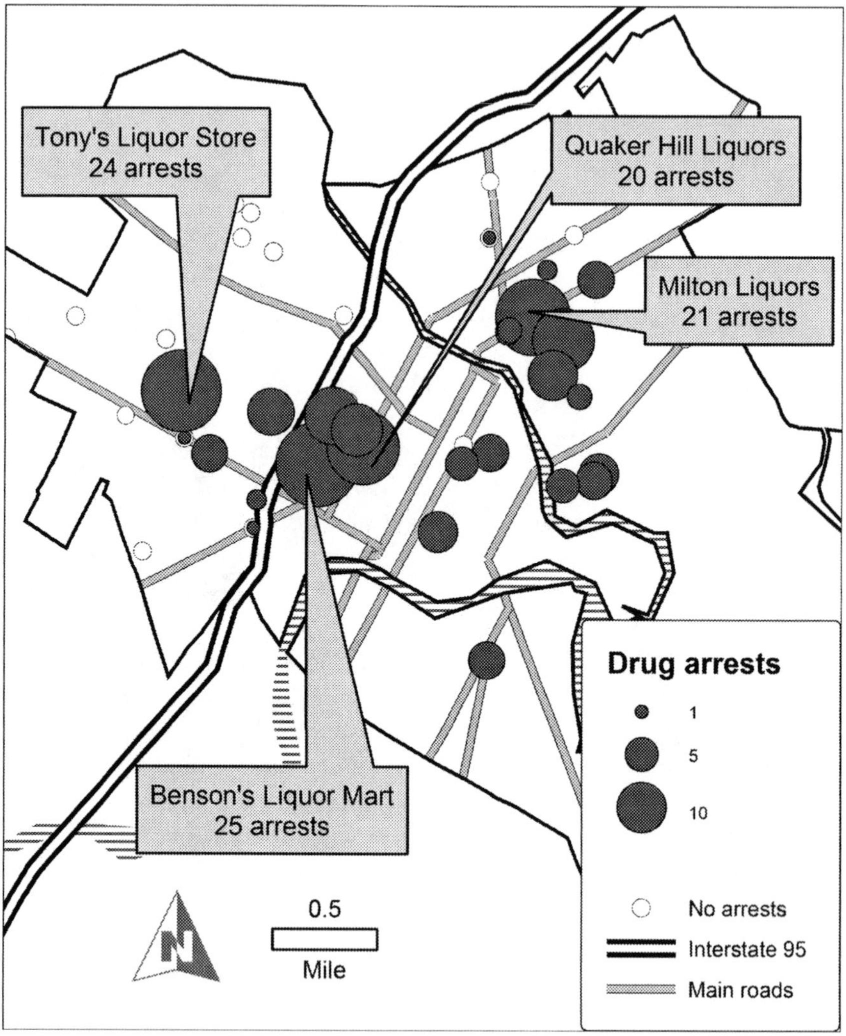

Tony's Liquor Store
24 arrests

Quaker Hill Liquors
20 arrests

Milton Liquors
21 arrests

Benson's Liquor Mart
25 arrests

Drug arrests

1

5

10

No arrests

Interstate 95

Main roads

0.5

Mile

Figure 7-3. Arrests within 400 Feet of Taverns: 1997

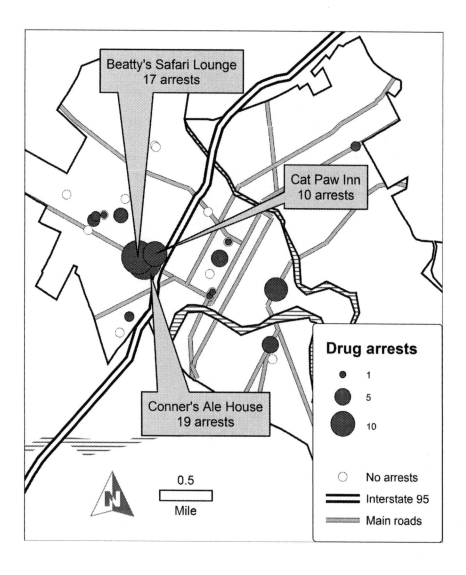

Beatty's Safari Lounge
17 arrests

Cat Paw Inn
10 arrests

Conner's Ale House
19 arrests

Drug arrests

- 1
- 5
- 10

○ No arrests

Interstate 95

Main roads

0.5
Mile

N

associated with or encouraging drug-market activity are not being solved. This brings into question whether or not a city can arrest its way out of illegal drug problems.

Are More Arrests the Answer?

The most recognized example of police attempting to arrest their way out of drug problems is termed a police crackdown. A police crackdown is when the police concentrate their forces on a localized site or community where drug dealing is prevalent. There have been both successes and lack-of-success stories when police crackdowns have been evaluated. Kleiman (1988) evaluated several of these attempts.

The first to be evaluated was a police crackdown on a drug market in Lynn, Massachusetts. This crackdown took the form of six state narcotics officers focusing on one community within Lynn. In this relatively small community, the police were able to reduce not only drug sales, but also property and violent crime. The same type of success was experienced in New York City with "Operation Pressure Point I" on the lower east side of Manhattan (Zimmer, 1987). From these examples, it would seem that both in a small and a large city a police crackdown met with success in the short term. However, when we examine a longer time frame, Barnett (1988) questions the success of the Lynn example. Evaluation studies must take into account more than a few years surrounding the crackdown if for no other reason than to smooth out yearly fluctuations in the data.

Police crackdowns were not successful in Lawrence, Massachusetts and Philadelphia, Pennsylvania (Kleiman, 1988). Again, we have a small and a large city evaluated, so city size is not what is important. The important difference between the successful and unsuccessful crackdowns seems to be the time frame of the analysis and the spatial focus of the crackdown. In Philadelphia, the police focused on the two worst drug corners in each of the city's 23 police districts. Termed "Operation Cold Turkey," the crackdown resulted in public protests and lawsuits. It only lasted four days. Lawrence, Massachusetts had a much larger drug market than Lynn, and police were being spread thinly over a larger area. Police crackdowns seem to work best when they have support from the local community and when they are focused on a well-defined area with sufficient police personnel. However, as Kleiman (1988) notes, the police will have to maintain a presence in the crackdown area if they are to keep the drug dealers from returning. This is not always economically or politically feasible.

Sherman (1990) identified a number of different reasons why police crackdowns generally do not achieve long-term crime reduction. These reasons included: crackdown decay (where the initial level of police involvement is reduced during the crackdown); initial deterrence decay (when offenders learn that they have over-estimated the chances of being detected); and residual deterrence decay (when the offenders eventually learn that the police action has ceased). Scott (2003) provides a summary of the effectiveness of crackdowns with a thorough and recent evaluation of the literature.

Changing the Local Economic Conditions of Drug Markets

Police crackdowns have not demonstrated long-term success when focused on illegal drug-market places. If and when the police leave a drug crackdown area, things tend to return to their previous state. This is because there are locational advantages to dealing drugs from that specific site. Therefore drug dealers will have an incentive to "snap back" to that location once the police leave the scene much like a rubber band snaps back to its former position once it is stretched and released. This snapping back implies that the characteristics of sites must be changed so that the sites are not attractive to drug dealers. In other words, remove or change the character of the anchor so that the rubber band is not attached but moved to another location. This does not necessarily imply stationing a police officer permanently at that location, as did the city of Philadelphia with its Safe Streets program (Wexler, 2003). Although a police officer's presence works to contain drug dealing, this is only effective for the duration of the officer's presence. As soon as the cop goes, drug dealing is likely to return because the underlying economic conditions that made that location viable for drug dealing have not been affected in any way.

Perhaps a police/community/government focus on identifying factors that encourage drug markets at a specific location could improve conditions. In other words, from the perspective of the police, they might practice "problem-oriented policing" as well as the "crime fighting" associated with crackdowns and making arrests. Having police make drug-related arrests without solving the problems related to the location where drugs are sold is the equivalent of parents spanking their children without solving the problems that led to the misbehavior in the first place. Children who are spanked without addressing the causes that led to the misbehavior are more likely to misbehave again. Likewise, arresting a drug dealer on a street corner is not likely to solve the problem of drug dealing at that location unless the very expensive tactic of operating police crackdowns or stationing an officer on a drug-dealing street corner most hours of the day is employed.

The ultimate problem is the demand for illegal drugs in our society. One often hears the statement that as long as there is a demand for illegal drugs, there will be a supply; i.e., someone selling illegal drugs. Clearly, education and treatment programs are of critical importance. But from a geographic and economic perspective, the statement that "as long as there is a demand, there will be a supplier" may be a bit too simplistic. Would (even a young) drug dealer stand on a corner all day waiting for a sale if s/he only made one small sale a day? Clearly not! A certain volume of sales (threshold conditions) must be met before sales will commence and continue from that corner. If this were not the case, why is there not a drug dealer on every corner of the city? Surely there will be some level of demand there sooner or later. The answer is that there are *best* places to sell illegal drugs because these are places where demand is focused spatially.

POLICY IMPLICATIONS OF THE MARKET ANALYSIS

Public policy should not ignore local demand for drugs. Rengert (1996) illustrates that even indoor dealing, which is less noxious than outdoor markets, can have an adverse effect on a community since the dealer cannot control the activities of drug users once they leave the establishment. By spatially aggregating the drug-dependent property offenders at a dealing location, the market also aggregates the related property and violent crimes that tend to focus on the immediate environment. Therefore, even seemingly unobtrusive drug dealers can harm the social fabric of a community by focusing crime within it. Localized demand for illegal drugs should not be ignored since it determines where a local marketplace will be profitable.

There are many tactics that focus on the local demand for illegal drugs. The most obvious is to establish effective treatment programs so that those who wish to kick the habit have a means of doing so. At present, there are not enough treatment programs (especially within our prison system) to meet demand. Furthermore, most are expensive, far beyond the ability of low-income inner-city residents to pay. Health insurance programs generally do not pay for the full extent of treatment required to break a drug dependency.

Public policy also should focus on the temporal dimension of addiction. A common feature of drug addiction is that it requires time to afford and enjoy illegal drugs (Rengert and Wasilchick, 1985). One means of curtailing the time available to experimenting drug users is to enact an effective school attendance policy. In other words, we should take school truancy seriously and provide meaningful education for urban as well as suburban and rural youth. This may require a more effective means of funding public education than reliance on local property taxes, in which low-income housing areas invariably have under-funded schools. It also may entail income transfers from more wealthy districts to inner-city schools. Note, again, the importance of national and local policy environments: the specific contexts of both truancy and funding sources for public education vary widely worldwide, and any generalization beyond the U.S. could only be misleading and uninformed.

A related antidote is an effective employment training program that again requires participants to devote time to their jobs, time that cannot be spent on illegal drug procurement and use. This is similar to an effective educational program, but goes further. Job training should be for jobs that are available in the post-industrial city. They will not be effective if they are "make work" jobs programs. The current *welfare to work* programs that are sweeping the United States have the goal of removing people from public assistance and moving them into gainful employment. However, if the available jobs are unattractive compared with those available in the informal economy (such as illegal drug sales), it is likely that many will not accept them (Fagan, 1993).

The best known tactic focused on blocking open-air drug markets, one that requires police-community cooperation, is the "weed and seed" program (Rengert, 1996). The *modus operandi* of this tactic is to plan a police sweep to rid a community of illegal drug dealers, combined with training local residents to assist the police in resisting the dealers' return. This tactic relies on effective cooperation between the police and residents of the community, among residents who may not be inclined to trust the police. If successful, there is a multiplier effect in that a given amount of police resources can be more successful than would occur in the absence of community cooperation. This "weed and seed" tactic has been applied in Wilmington without measurable success (Bostrom, 2000). However, better results have been experienced in other cities. Clearly, research is required before weed and seed is accepted as a panacea.

Finally, the anti-drug campaigns in the local and national media need to target potential users more effectively than has been the case in the past. Many of these radio and television spots have been written without research on what matters most to potential drug users, especially youth. The ads have tended to focus on health issues, which concern youth less than they do the middle-aged copy writers who create these media campaigns. In the post-9/11 world, some advertising has even tried to suggest that marijuana use supports terrorism (though this claim is rather hard to sustain given that a significant amount of marijuana is grown within North America). These advertisements lack a fundamental understanding of the drug-using community they are trying to influence. Recently, these ads have changed their focus onto social acceptance, a major concern of many youth. Using popular sports figures also is more likely to maintain the attention of potential users than ads that use a person from the streets who tells of the dangers of drug abuse. But young people soon become tired and bored by the same old ads, even if they are carefully crafted. New and fresh approaches must be aired either weekly or biweekly to maintain the attention of youth.

Why Place is the Key

If we take the best places away from the drug dealers, they must then sell at second or third best places. An argument is often made that it does no good to close a drug market place since it will simply reopen a block or two away (Bauza, 1988). In other words, spatial displacement will occur (MacNamara, 1994). The problem with the phrase "it does no good" is that it overlooks the economic and geographic principles associated with making drug dealers operate from suboptimal (second or third choice) places. As pointed out by Kleiman (1988) and Knutsson (2000), spatial displacement increases the effort involved in locating a source of drugs, which, in turn, reduces demand. In sum, it takes profit out of the hands of drug dealers. In fact, spatial displacement is a good thing, not a bad thing. If we can move dealers from their best locations, we should affect the amount of drugs consumed (Kleiman, 1988).

The question now turns on where the best places to sell drugs are in Wilmington and perhaps in other cities. The answer is twofold. First, the location-allocation analysis in Chapter 4 demonstrated that illicit drugs tend to be sold in neighborhoods where there is a local demand within an acceptable range associated with the demographic profile of the residents. This is in communities where a disproportionate percentage of the residents living nearby are either young, or high school dropouts or unemployed. The statistical analysis in chapter 6 expanded on this analysis to demonstrate that drug-sales arrests tended to be concentrated in minority communities with vacant homes and in communities with many female-headed households with children under five. Drug-sales arrests were negatively associated with renter-occupied units.

The second factor associated with where drugs are sold in Wilmington involves built environmental features that spatially aggregate potential customers. In the analysis using location quotients, several of these features were identified. And in the statistical analysis, most of these factors were in fact related to where illegal drugs are sold in Wilmington. But not all built features of the environments that serve as destinations of the routine activities of potential drug users were found to be associated with drug-sales arrests. Social service centers and taverns were negatively associated with drug-sales arrest volume.

There are two features that are commonly associated with drug markets: schools (Rengert and Chakravorty, 1995) and transportation interchanges (Levine et al., 1986; Levine and Wachs, 1986; Loukaitou-Sideris et al., 2002). We have already examined the somewhat distinctive situations surrounding Wilmington schools, where most students are bused or frequently driven to suburban schools for desegregation reasons. Therefore, there is no spatial aggregation of students walking to school to provide a potential market for drug dealers on the streets surrounding the schools. Few students are found on the streets surrounding schools in Wilmington.

The second feature commonly associated with illegal drug market places is the presence of rapid rail and bus stations. Neither the Amtrak station in Wilmington nor the bus stations are statistically associated with drug-sales arrests. This is a surprising finding. However, drug customers are served near certain exit ramps of a limited-access highway, once a drug market has been established. The areas near the exit ramps of limited access highways have been determined to be associated with illegal drug sales in past research (Robinson, 2003). Interstate I-95 bisects the city of Wilmington and is associated both with the existence and with the size of illegal drug markets. However, there is not a lot more Wilmington can do to change this situation. In Wilmington, exit and entry ramps to I-95 are not located near each other. Regional customers of illegal drug markets prefer a "drive through" situation, much like a fast food franchise. But in Wilmington, one must drive for many blocks from an exit ramp before finding an entry ramp. This explains why the highest location quotients were not within three blocks of an exit ramp. The only variable positively associated with the size of an illegal drug market in Wilmington was a location between three and four blocks of an I-95 exit. As the first part of the ZIP model analysis showed, this requires a market to be in existence. Over all, therefore, one can say that where a market exists, the exits work to increase the size of a market. Where a market does not exist, the exits work to increase the chance of a market not developing. As with taverns, it appears that there are good and bad freeway exits.

Where they exist, the large illegal drug markets were not next to the exits where cars are speeding off the ramps, but a few blocks away where regional customers could feel comfortable buying illegal drugs. Although illegal drug-sales arrests were very high in many of the blocks surrounding these exits, they were highest in the three- to four-block range. In short, there is not a lot more the city of Wilmington can do to discourage drug sales associated with its interstate highway. However, other cities, especially those just building a major highway, may wish to consider the example of Wilmington. In fact, some cities are using barriers to create a Wilmington-type situation (Graham and Ott, 2004; Reuter and MacCoun, 1992), and the Institute of Transportation Engineers has a website dedicated to the "state of the art" of traffic calming (www.ite.org/traffic).

The problem associated with illicit drug markets that service regional customers from outside the city is their relative accessibility. Interstate highways funnel suburban residents into fertile grounds for purchasing illegal drugs. Graham and Ott (2004:B-6) describe such a situation in Camden, New Jersey:

> For a variety of reasons, the Alley, in particular, has proved to be fertile ground for drug dealing. Just off Baird and Admiral Wilson Boulevards, the Alley provided easy access for suburban customers.

Some residents in the Alley were paid $100 a day to stash drugs, which were moved regularly between the units. The confined fortress-like path between Boyd and Morse made it difficult for police to watch undetected.

In the case of Wilmington, the interstate highway leading through the city is associated with a concentration of drug-sales arrests in both the location quotient analysis and the statistical analysis. There are several tactics designed to make open-air drug markets less accessible to people who do not reside in the community. Since it is not feasible to eliminate the exits from interstate highways in a city, one tactic is to rearrange street patterns so that illegal drug markets are less accessible from the exits. Commuters like easy in-and-out routes akin to drive-through restaurants. A tactic to make access less easy is to establish or change the pattern of one-way streets. This can be accomplished by designating a series of three or more streets as one-way conduits onto the feeder route rather than having them lead toward a drug-market place. If the commuter is required to drive four or more blocks before he or she can exit a feeder route, the commuter will spend more time, and feel less secure, traveling through an often strange and potentially hostile neighborhood.

A related tactic is to establish a series of dead-end streets leading from the feeder highway. Again, non-residents will feel less comfortable buying illegal drugs in an area where they are required to spend time attempting to turn around to get back on the feeder road and the interstate. This tactic is termed the St. Louis Private Street Plan (Newman, 1973). It is essentially the same as creating cul-de-sacs (of the type that suburban residents enjoy in their neighborhoods) in the city. It has been determined that this type of street is less crime-prone than one that has many avenues of egress (Bevis and Nutter, 1977).

Another tactic that focuses on the non-resident who purchases drugs in the city, a tactic that more directly involves the local police, is to arrest the buyer and require him to forfeit the vehicle used to make the purchase. This practice was termed "Operation Fishnet" in Philadelphia. It is designed to discourage commuters from entering urban neighborhoods to purchase drugs. However, there are many problems associated with this tactic. These include the potential and often probable confiscation of borrowed vehicles or vehicles belonging to a company rather than to the drug-purchasing individual. Also, it has been the past practice of the police is to keep the operation a secret from the public so that more cars can be confiscated before the public becomes aware of this possibility. A better tactic to discourage the commuters from driving into drug-market places is to advertise beforehand that cars will be confiscated from those who drive into a community to purchase drugs, and then to carry out the tactic, perhaps on a random-time basis. Secrecy can be punitive but cannot simultaneously be a deterrent.

Homeless shelters also seem to have drug dealing under control in their surrounding areas. There are fewer drug sales on the block where these facilities are located than a block away. They cannot be expected to control areas beyond one city block from their facility. However, this is where drug-sales arrests tend to cluster in Wilmington. The area just over one block from a homeless shelter was a significant predictor of drug market size.

The difference between liquor stores and taverns is interesting. Wieczorek and Coyle (1996) discovered more assaults within 300 feet of off-premise alcohol outlets than on-premise outlets. This suggests more control of the environment by managers of on-premise locations than liquor stores, a finding mirrored in our study. In the present analysis, taverns were found to be inversely associated with the number of drug-sales arrests when the central part of the city was analyzed (the masked city). Only those taverns that happened to be located where drug-sales arrests were clustered were associated with, but not necessarily the cause of, drug-sales arrests (see Figure 7-3). These taverns were clustered in susceptible neighborhoods near I-95 exits.

Liquor stores, on the other hand, were statistically associated with the growth of drug-sales arrests in both the masked city and the entire city. They tended to have many more drug-sales arrests on their blocks and near their establishments than taverns. Liquor stores associated with drug-sales arrests also seemed to be more spatially dispersed than taverns. The difference between taverns and liquor stores is intriguing. Perhaps the difference is associated with the level of guardianship associated with each. Tavern owners and bar tenders are responsible for the behavior of their customers, who may spend hours in their establishments. Liquor stores, on the other hand, only interact with customers for a few minutes as they purchase a bottle and leave the establishment. Many drug users enjoy poly drug use, mixing alcohol with illegal drugs in the same episode. This can best be done off-premises by buying a bottle and consuming it along with illegal drugs in a neighboring site – perhaps a local park, empty lot, or alley way. Again, it may not be the liquor store that is the problem, but rather where it is situated with respect to conditions drug users find desirable.

These are conditions or problem areas that the police, community and government officials may address. For example, should liquor stores be located next to public parks and playgrounds? Knutsson (2000) found that local authorities could clean up a municipal park by removing drug users from their favorite locations within a park. More directly, just as taverns and liquor stores are zoned away from schools, liquor stores could be zoned away from community parks and playgrounds, making it less handy for drug users to purchase and consume drugs nearby.

Another condition often used by drug users is a neighborhood containing abandoned homes. These locations provide a fertile ground to sell and use drugs out of sight of the local police or community residents. One solution to this problem is to knock down abandoned properties that no longer have a legitimate economic use. For example, Graham and Ott (2004:B1-2) note how Camden, New Jersey is attempting to take back a notorious open-air drug market with the help of the City Department of Public Works;

> Twenty derelict houses along a former drug market known as the Alley are to be demolished today in Camden. The 10-year drug operation . . . made millions of dollars and had ties to the mob and City Hall. . . . Projects such as demolishing the Alley and replacing a once thriving drug market with homes are essential to bringing change to the neighborhoods, leaders say. The only thing that can be said after a long time of just horrible conditions . . . is something fresh and bright has to grow.

On the other hand, some cities have experimented with zoning areas where drug dealing is concentrated as a "Drug Free Zone" (DFZ). Robinson (2003) examined the case of Portland, Oregon, where several DFZs were established. Legislation was passed that enabled the police to charge any person known to have been convicted of a drug offense with trespassing if s/he entered one of these zones for reasons other than work, school or residential purposes. In other words, drug offenders were zoned away from these areas of the city.

In her evaluation of Portland's DFZ ordinances, Robinson (2003) discovered that the legislation (laws) did not have a significant direct effect. But the legislation provided police administrators with a reason to concentrate police officers in the drug-free zones. And the concentration of police in fact did have a significant impact on the spatial location of drug dealers. In the next chapter, additional examples of police practices focused on illegal drug dealing are discussed.

8. REDUCING THE IMPACT OF STREET-LEVEL DRUG MARKETS

In this final chapter, we consider a variety of approaches to addressing local drug markets.

It is often asserted that national and local officials should concentrate on reducing the demand for illegal drugs by rehabilitating addicts with treatment programs (as discussed in Chapter 7). Another view is that local police can focus on local drug markets by making as many arrests as possible to reduce the supply and availability of drugs. However, the latter approach suggests that local police can arrest their way out of drug problems. A punitive solution is much too simple. Reuter (1997:275), for example, highlights the idea that being less punitive may be preferable to being more punitive:

> Doing less rarely attracts much support for dealing with a problem that still concerns large parts of the community. . . . Locking up drug offenders for shorter terms, worrying more about the racial disparities in sentencing policies, giving up fewer of our civil liberties for unlikely reductions in drug problems, may be the best one can do at the moment. That means less intrusive, divisive, and expensive policies and perhaps little increase in drug problems.

The police cannot solve local drug problems by simply making more arrests. We see in Wilmington that the police are making arrests year after year in the same areas, yet drug dealers keep coming back to these areas because they are the best places to sell illegal drugs. Perhaps Reuter (1997) is correct in stating that less is better. Rather than focusing on arresting drug offenders, our argument is that the police and other local officials should focus on what creates the demand for illegal drugs and why this demand is centered spatially in certain sites within urban areas. In other words, what are the local contextual factors that make a drug market area attractive from an economic perspective?

We have described the economic nature of local drug markets and the financial forces that drive the complicated relationship between customer availability and the market provider. The case study of Wilmington illustrates that drug markets do not involve random locations selected by drug offenders, but are the result of an interaction of economic, social and structural factors. In this final chapter, the role of local police in tackling this problem is discussed.

IS GIS THE EASY ANSWER?

The first task of a police department is to understand the scope of the problem. That is to say, police should understand the temporal, methodological (from a criminal perspective), and most importantly, spatial dimensions of the drug market. Geographic Information Systems (GIS) would seem to be an easy solution to this part of the problem. To anyone new to the field of crime analysis, it might appear that GIS are now integral to the work of the police in many areas. It is understandable how this impression could appear. In the U.K., the National Intelligence Model asks analysts to explore crime and disorder hot spots. In the U.S., the U.S. federal National Institute of Justice has a Mapping and Analysis for Public Safety (MAPS) program, which disseminates free software and publications.

Mapping systems are now mainstream business applications for police in many other countries. It is worth remembering that this was not always the case. In the U.K., where the enthusiasm to laud success is often tempered by a bit more honesty than in the U.S, there have been times when GIS implementation has been thoroughly unsuccessful. Stan Openshaw and colleagues (1990) recount the lack of success in trying to integrate GIS into the crime management thinking of the Northumbria Police (U.K.) in the late 1980s, citing a number of reasons, including failures on the part of the users, failures on the part of the system vendors, and a range of general problems only some of which will have been overcome due to the passage of time and the increase in computer processing and printing speeds.

Ken Pease (2001) similarly recounts the sorry tale of a Crime Analysis Package (CAPGEN software) that was distributed by the U.K. Home Office Crime Prevention Centre from 1989 to 1991. The mapping facility was integrated into the spreadsheet part of the program, and while there were some crime reduction successes attributed to the spreadsheet component, the mapping aspect was never fully utilized in any of the police divisions that ran the program. Whenever Pease visited a police station and saw the software demonstrated, he was shown the demonstration maps that were included with the software. None of the sites that used the program had developed their own mapping ability. He concluded that "either the system was not sufficiently user-friendly, or the enterprise itself was flawed" (Pease, 2001:226).

Clearly, there is a danger of police departments entering into the potentially time-consuming and expensive venture that GIS crime mapping can be without any clear idea of what they hope to achieve from the exercise, and without any clear idea of how it can help them. Neil Quarmby (2004) recently wrote about the value of looking forward in the thinking of law enforcement. He outlined three basic criteria that had to be satisfied before there was any value in running a strategic intelligence exercise, namely:

- There is an identifiable decision-making system to support.

- There is a will to think ahead in both intelligence and the decision-making system.

- There is a will to apply results in both intelligence and the decision-making system.

There would seem to be an overlap in thinking between criteria for a strategic intelligence unit and a GIS mapping system. Before embarking on the training of personnel, the purchase of computers and mapping systems, the further purchase of base digital maps, and the possible adaptation of existing crime and call-for-service recording mechanisms for GIS compatibility, police executives should ask themselves:

- Is there an identifiable decision-making system to support?

- Is there a will to employ spatial analysis before decisions are made?

- Is there a will to allow decisions to be influenced by GIS analysis?

There is an assumption that decision-making systems are clear within law enforcement. However, evidence would often suggest otherwise. Ratcliffe (2005) found that crime and intelligence analysts were often unclear as to the client for intelligence products that they created, and that their view of the client was often at odds with the view of the police executives. In other words, nobody really knew who was making the crime reduction decisions. In the end, many analysts concentrated their efforts on the street level officers. Unfortunately, these officers were not accountable for the information they received and there was little incentive for them to act upon intelligence passed to them. They could choose whether or not to undertake discretionary activities, such as pursuing intelligence leads. As noted by one crime analyst (Ratcliffe, 2005): "[There is a] lack of responsibility. It is better to go through the supervisor to get accountability."

There is also evidence that planning and decisions are often divorced from the available intelligence and analysis. It is often lost on police executives that middle management and operational commanders may require training and education in the interpretation of crime maps. The assumption is that by virtue of having been a police officer for a while, an operational commander will know how to interpret a map of crime distribution and will also know what to do about the mapped crime problem. This would be a more reasonable assumption if police officers were all trained in problem-oriented policing, however that is far from the case. Table 8-1 shows the number of training days dedicated to different policing strands in the training programs available from the International Association of Chiefs of Police (IACP) in 2004. The catalogue lists all of the programs offered across

Table 8-1. Main Categories of Programs Offered in the 2004 IACP Training Catalogue

Program category	Number of courses offered
Quality Leadership	5
Community Involvement	58
Management and Supervision	12
Crisis Management	53
Force Management and Integrity Issues	58
Staffing, Personnel and Legal Issues	59
Patrol Operations and Tactical Responses	13
Investigations	10

Source: (Ratcliffe, 2004a).

the U.S. (www.iacp.org/training/-2004IACPTrainingCatalog.pdf), comprising 68 different programs organized into categories. The main categories are listed in Table 8-1.

Only one of the 68 courses provides any training to police executives in the areas of problem-oriented policing, intelligence-led policing or general crime prevention and reduction. There are no categories dedicated to problem-oriented policing, and indeed there is little that bears any relation to crime reduction. This is not intended as a direct criticism of the IACP. Far from it: the IACP offers the most widely accepted programs available to police chiefs in the U.S., and they are simply responding to user demand. It simply would appear that there is no perceived need among police chiefs to remain current with the latest crime reduction information.

In the New Zealand case study (Ratcliffe, 2005), the unclear decision-making structure resulted in comments from crime analysts like the following about an intelligence officer's relationship with the district commander: "There isn't one. There is no consultation, he is too [non-crime] performance focused." In three police districts, not one single crime analyst saw the district commander as a client for intelligence products. In a situation such as this, even if crime maps could show the patterns of street drug markets, they would be unlikely to be utilized by the management, which did not see crime analysts as performing a tactical function. As one analyst said: "Here there is a risk and performance manager, and a performance analyst. We haven't done tactical intelligence; we have done performance appraisal work" (Ratcliffe, 2005). Many law enforcement agencies are unwilling to focus resources on hot spots, and seem to have a point of view concerning mapping and the geography of crime that is summed up nicely by Irene Reed in her blues song, *If You Are Aiming at Nothing, You Will Hit it Every Time.*

Finally, the successful use of GIS goes beyond simply producing maps for management meetings: those maps should influence thinking and have an impact on the decision making of crime reduction practitioners. This requires that decision makers can convert a two-dimensional map of crime into a concrete crime reduction program that is evidence-based and targeted to the right place at the right time. For example, Ratcliffe (2004b), discusses the need for influence and impact through a 3i model.

It is interesting to speculate how many police departments have implemented a crime mapping system without any real clear idea of what it would achieve, and how many simply assumed that the benefits would be tangible immediately. More information in color formats does not mean less crime. Information has to be translated into crime reduction tactics: unfortunately, while maps identify the problem areas, crime maps do not tell a police chief what to do about the problem. This requires going beyond the maps to identify the spatial and environmental context of a crime site.

While we strongly advocate that police departments acquire the ability to map the incidence of crime, we also feel that police departments should be clear about the benefits, limitations and costs (both financial and in personnel terms) that can result from adoption of mapping technology. We feel that the benefits far outweigh the costs, but a realistic understanding of the mapping process will prevent overestimating the value of a mapping system. As Read and Oldfield (1995:29) note: " . . . bearing in mind the likely cost of a GIS system it is important that police forces plan how the GIS component will be used in analysis, and what its benefits are likely to be, before investing in such a system." A GIS is not a "silver bullet." It is a valuable weapon in the arsenal of the police, if used properly. So how should GIS be used "properly" in the context of illegal drug markets? A thorough treatment of the steps required to set up and operate a crime mapping system can be found in Chainey and Ratcliffe (in press).

MAPPING THE SPATIAL CONTEXT
OF DRUG PROBLEMS

What we have shown in the analysis presented earlier in this book is that the spatial context is important to understanding the distribution of drug problems. But the spatial context we analyzed is very limited in scope. One should not come to a "knee jerk" conclusion that, for example, all liquor stores and/or taverns are a negative influence on the neighborhoods where they are situated. It may be, for instance, that certain neighborhoods are a bad influence on the liquor stores and/or taverns that are located within them.

For short-term policing applications, it may be sufficient to simply map the incidence of drug activity as recorded by the police. For many police departments this will be both challenging and rewarding. However, a more detailed understanding of drug-market dynamics will be enhanced by considering a broader range of data services. Pease (2001) made the claim for the integration of a spatial analysis with non-spatial variables, even though many of the variables he suggests for inclusion have a spatial component. We would not argue with this; the inclusion of non-crime spatial variables will help police better define the problem that they face in a problem-oriented scenario.

Although we suggested that simply mapping the incidence of drug activity will have value, this value will only exist in a short-term sense. This is for two reasons. First, recorded information on drug activity is influenced by police activity. In other words, by concentrating on an area of past drug arrests, police run the risk of creating a self-fulfilling prophecy whereby future policing priorities will be determined by past police activity. Second, by excluding all information except police activity incidents, there may be a tendency to assume that a policing response is always the most appropriate. Thus, if an area has a high arrest rate, then surely more arrests are needed? Well, this is not necessarily true, for the following reasons.

Any police strategy that relies solely on a law enforcement response will eventually run into problems. This is why a law enforcement response is only a short-term solution. Police cannot arrest their way out of illegal drug problems in their jurisdictions. Increased patrols and arrests do not get to the root cause of a crime problem. Further, this strategy places the police in a situation where continued presence is required to maintain a level of crime control. Police in such situations often complain that as soon as they leave, the drug market will return. There is a clear tendency for drug markets to "snap back" to the most advantageous location. As we demonstrated in the earlier chapters, they are probably correct about this, because the drug market exists in a particular location for sound economic reasons: it is the best place to deal illicit drugs! Police may succeed in temporarily moving dealers to a less attractive location, or force them to convert to an indoor market; but a particular site or street corner will still be the best place to deal from, and there will be economic reasons to return to that location as soon as police patrols ease up. This tendency of drug dealers to "snap back" to advantaged locations is described by Graham and Ott (2004:B-6) who quote the experience of neighbors of an illegal drug market in Camden, New Jersey: "It's like spraying roaches. You have to spray over and over."

A long-term solution will require more than "spraying" again and again. A change in the economic and/or physical conditions that make a location attractive to drug dealers is what is required. Until then, arrests will often continue and police will have to continue making that location a priority patrol. Long-term solutions require a problem-oriented policing solution that examines the underlying influences in the social-spatial context of the drug market location. This requires mapping or otherwise identifying non-crime features of the urban mosaic, in addition to crime features, and testing their influence on drug activity.

Kleiman and Young (1995:730) list the components of a drug-market place that they term factors of production: " . . . a common venue; the buyers' access to the venue, desire for drugs, income, and perceived chance of impunity; and the sellers' labor, operating scope within the venue, supply of drugs, ways to spend or save money earned, and perceived chance of impunity." They define the optimal strategy to confront this situation as one that concentrates on those factors that can most readily be made scarce relative to the others: they term this a limiting factor of production. We would add to this list a desirable place nearby where the buyer can enjoy the illegal drugs they purchased. This is especially the case for local buyers who arrive on foot. The police and other city officials need to understand the nature of places where these factors of production come together to form drug markets.

In this book we are especially concerned with the venues of drug sales and with the buyers' access to this venue that is fixed in space. This does not address door-to-door sales or office delivery, which are becoming more common in many urban areas (Curtis and Wendel, 1998). Venues that are fixed in space may be divided between those that are indoor and those that are outdoor. Table 8-2, taken from Kleiman and Young (1995:735), lists tactics focused on indoor sales locations. Although many of these tactics do not involve the police directly, police using a problem-oriented approach can facilitate most of these tactics by contacting the appropriate agency in the local government or initiating procedures in other forms. The important lesson is that police look beyond their traditional mission of making arrests to identify more long-term solutions. Examples of these tactics are provided below.

Some of these measures are controversial and others may be unproductive, such as the boarding up of abandoned properties. In the previous chapter we found that vacant property was significantly associated with illegal drug-sales arrests. This is because drug dealers can easily

Table 8-2.   Tactics Focused on Indoor Sales of Illegal Drugs

1. If a property is owned by a public authority:
   a. Boarding up or demolishing vacant buildings.
   b. Redesigning apartment houses to eliminate corridors.
   c. Locking external doors to apartment buildings.
   d. Evicting dealers.

2. If a property is privately owned:
   a. Nuisance abatement.[1]
   b. "Bawdy-house" laws.[2]
   c. Code enforcement.[3]
   d. Forfeiture or threat of forfeiture.[4]

gain access to boarded-up properties, often even when reinforced metal is used to block access. More important, boarding up abandoned buildings make them more of an "eyesore" than they previously were. They are a sign that this is a drug-dealing neighborhood. In short, they increase signs of incivility that exist in the neighborhood. It is better to tear down the abandoned property and turn it into a neighborhood garden or play area. Or, if the whole block contains abandoned properties, they can be torn down and new construction built to invigorate the neighborhood (Graham and Ott, 2004). Leaving the abandoned properties in any form in a neighborhood creates problems beyond illegal drug sales. Most important, it is not making good use of valuable urban infrastructure.

As an example, Kennedy (1990) notes that the razing of some abandoned buildings was crucial to the successful elimination of drug dealers from the formerly crack-infested Link Valley neighborhood of Houston. In a later study, Kennedy (1993) found that razing abandoned buildings in Tampa accomplished little, until it was combined with other tactics developed by the highly effective Quick Uniform Attack on Drugs (QUAD) Program. For example, a city code enforcement officer was assigned to the QUAD program. This resulted in the closure of many drug-dealing locations. What is important to note here is that "one size does not fit all." Also, one tactic may not be sufficient to eliminate a problem. Effective tactics may be unique to specific communities. Police are in an excellent position to identify these unique tactics.

The tactic of evicting drug dealers from their homes or apartments is controversial. This is because the eviction generally includes not only the drug offender, but also the immediate family. For example, a teenage drug dealer may be detected selling drugs outside the public housing complex where he lives with his grandmother and sisters. The question is whether the grandmother and sisters should be evicted because the dealer is arrested. This tactic results in a situation where the policy makes individuals not guilty of a crime (as well as the guilty party) suffer sanctions.

Table 8-3 taken from Kleiman and Young (1995:737), lists tactics targeting the buyers'-side factors in the production of a drug market. Again, some of these measures can be controversial. Law-abiding citizens and residents of communities may resent the inconvenience involved in closing or changing street patterns. Emergency vehicle operators, such fire and ambulance services, may feel that these tactics reduce response time. But others champion these tactics. For example Cose (1994) documents how a grid pattern of streets in the Five Oaks community of Dayton, Ohio was subdivided into 10 separate cul-de-sac neighborhoods, similar to those enjoyed by suburban residents. This resulted in a 67% reduction in traffic flow. As Bevis and Nutter (1977) determined, reduced access translates into less crime. In the case of drug dealers, it translates into fewer customers.

Finally, Kleiman and Young (1995:741-742) list tactics focused on factors of production from the sellers' perspective. Table 8-4 lists these tactics.

The tactics listed in tables 8-2 through 8-4 represent close to an exhaustive list of policies that may affect drug dealers directly and/or indirectly. Many of these policies are beyond the reach of the police to control directly. For example, police cannot increase jail/prison capacity even if this would be an effective policy concerning illegal drug sales. They also must be careful not to encourage programs that are of questionable value, such as source-country policies. However, they can use many of the other policies in conjunction with traditional law enforcement functions to address illegal drug sales. For example, the police can work with citizens' groups to address illegal drug sales. They can cooperate with other city agencies to enforce health and safety codes. They can encourage public works departments to clean up overgrown lots and parks. In other words, the police can identify what

Table 8-3.   Tactics Focused on Buyers of Illegal Drugs

1.   Access to venue:
    a.   Parking and traffic enforcement.[5]
    b.   Blocking off streets or changing them to one-way streets.
    c.   Checkpoints.[6]
    d.   Door attendants in housing projects.
    e.   Picket signs and bullhorns used by anti-drug citizens' groups.[7]

2.   Desire for drugs:
    a.   Anti-drug messages (school, media, neighborhood).
    b.   Treatment (including maintenance).

3.   Income:
    a.   Target hardening of property-crime targets.[8]
    b.   Anti-prostitution efforts.[9]
    c.   Drug testing for employees and benefit recipients.
    d.   Restitution orders for drug-involved offenders.[10]

4.   Buyers' sense of impunity:
    a.   "Sell-and-bust" operations (increased undercover activity).[11]
    b.   Sales of "turkey dope."[12]
    c.   Observation arrests.[13]
    d.   Questioning suspected market participants.
    e.   Picket signs and bullhorns used by anti drug citizens' groups.
    f.   Seizure and forfeiture of vehicles.
    g.   Car checks and postcards.[14]
    h.   Drug testing for drug-involved offenders.
    i.   Drug testing for employees and benefit recipients.
    j.   Fines.
    k.   Publicity.[15]

problems exist on the site and address these problems using any combination of the above policies. But first, the police must identify where illegal drug markets are located.

There are several GIS software programs that can identify the spatial clustering of illegal drug markets. These are often termed "hot spot" analyses. They identify spatial clustering in general terms over the study area. They do not directly answer specific questions such as, "what are the drug offense clusters clustered around?" For example, police and prosecutors often wish to determine, for legal reasons, whether a drug

Table 8-4. Tactics to Target Sellers of Illegal Drugs

1. Operating scope:
   a. Towing cars.
   b. Cutting brush.
   c. Lighting.[16]
   d. Door attendants in housing projects.
   e. Antigun measures (seizures and gun control).

2. Drug supply:
   a. Crop eradication.
   b. Source-country law enforcement.
   c. Interdiction.
   d. Long-term undercover operations.
   e. Historical investigation of drug conspiracies.
   f. Electronic surveillance.
   g. Financial investigation.
   h. High-level supplier enforcement.
   i. "Buy-and-bust" operations.
   j. "Working-up-the-chain" investigations.
   k. Control of intermediate chemicals and diluting agents.

3. Incentive:
   a. Denying saving opportunity.
      i. Money-laundering investigations.
      ii. Seizures and forfeitures.
      iii. Civil suits.
      iv. Fines.

4. Denying spending opportunity:
   a. Tax investigation.
   b. Checking ownership records of jewelry and cars.[17]
   c. Dress codes for students, probationers, and parolees.
   d. Forfeitures.[18]
   e. Fines.

5. Labor:
   a. Job programs to divert labor to licit markets.
   b. Sanctions for lookouts.[19]
   c. Penalties for using minors.
   d. "Working-up-the-chain" investigations.
   e. Prosecution of minor gang-related crimes.
   f. Field interrogation.[20]
   g. Boys' Clubs and athletic leagues.

Table 8-4. *(continued)*

6. Sellers' impunity:
   a. "Buy-and-bust" operations.[21]
   b. Observation arrests.
   c. Citizen hot lines.
   d. Searches.
   e. Special prosecution policies.
   f. Forfeitures.
   g. Eviction s.
   h. More jail/prison capacity.
   i. Special penalties for armed dealers.
   j. More capacity for non prison sanctions.
   k. Non criminal punishments.
   l. Finding and using fingerprints.
   m. Electronic surveillance.
   n. Beat cops.[22]
   o. Work with citizens' groups.
   p. Questioning suspected market participants.
   q. Mandatory abstinence and urine monitoring.

arrest is within 1,000 feet of a school. And, analysts may wish to identify other features around which drug dealing may be clustered, such as public parks and playgrounds. This requires other methods some of which are simple to use and easy to understand.

Analytical techniques such as location quotients (see Chapter 5) can help a police department understand the clustering of offenses near certain urban features. Location quotients are relatively simple to calculate and can be done in modern GIS without the purchase of additional software. We suggest that analysts undertake their own analyses in their local areas, because the local socio-spatial context may differ in areas other than Wilmington.

For police departments wishing to encourage long-term crime reduction, an understanding of the broader context of drug markets would appear essential. Without this understanding, crime prevention will rely on preventive patrolling and arrests, strategies that are short term and expensive. Longer-term strategies explore the possibilities of changing the socio-economics of drug markets in order to make the economics of running an illegal drug market in that location financially unviable. These strategies come with the advantage of rarely requiring a long-term law enforcement commitment, an idea attractive to both street-level officers and city budget masters. GIS can therefore provide a more complete picture of the immediate vicinity of a drug market, both in terms of the crime distribution as well as the social, access and opportunity structures.

PROBLEM SOLVING WITHIN LOCAL DRUG MARKETS

Drugs are a pervasive problem in the United States, a problem that will not be controlled with simple solutions. Although problem-oriented policing appears to be simple, solving the problem of illegal drug markets requires careful consideration of a range of complex factors, factors that often have an interactional component. Unfortunately as Eck (2004:189) states in relation to problem-oriented policing in general: "it is obvious from reviewing problem-solving efforts in these countries [United States, Great Britain, Canada] that few police agencies go beyond a shallow exploration of problems to examine creative methods for addressing them." Nevertheless, there have been some successes in regard to local drug markets.

Sampson and Scott (1999) provide a number of illustrative examples of problem-oriented policing solutions to street drug markets that do not rely only on arrests. In the Delray Beach, Florida example discussed previously, the problem facing police officers was not insubstantial, and is described thus (Sampson and Scott, 1999:23):

> ... Mario's Market was open on all sides. No fencing surrounded the property. A drug house behind the store contributed to the problem. The tenants, relatively recent move-ins, would sell drugs in front of and, sometimes, in the store; they would run back to their house if officers were active in the area. The T-shaped alley behind the store provided easy ingress and egress for buyers, both on foot and in cars. A shady tree grew in front of the store, providing cover, and a trash receptacle under it provided a place to rest alcoholic beverages. The lighting was poor, the phones out front were a home-away-from-home for dealers, and the indoor video games provided night-and-day entertainment for those engaged in crime.

In response, police went far beyond simply making drug-dealing arrests. They started a nuisance-abatement suit against the owner of the drug house, organized the putting in place of no trespassing signs, blocked off part of the alley with barriers, moved the trash dumpster into the sun (to deter dealers wanting to sit on it), repaired a chain link fence, added a reinforced light, painted the corner store and installed a fake video camera. The police did not do all these things themselves; they made sure that they were done. As Sampson and Scott report, the police were successful in turning around this drug corner. What is noticeable about this success story is two things. First, although this required some effort from the police, the success has been long term and has not required significant police involvement for the whole of that time. Note that among all of the police activities mentioned, arrests were not a significant factor in eventual success. Second, the factor that negates the need for police patrol commitment is that the officers worked to make the location physically and thus economically unviable for the drug community. In other words, to deal drugs at that location became so difficult it was no longer a profitable enterprise.

In another example, from Portland, Oregon, the initial police response would be predictable for anyone reading the earlier chapters of this book. The officers made several dozen arrests, but the impact was fleeting: the dealers found out the officers' shift and arranged their dealing for times when officers were off duty. As a result, the officers altered their shifts, but "soon realized that [they] were just spinning [their] wheels" (Sampson and Scott, 1999:29). Only when they began to tackle the root causes of the problem, by considering the attractiveness of the site for drug activity, did they begin to have success. In this case, police were at the heart of a multi-agency approach that saw one building leveled, a shack dismantled and the surrounding vegetation removed, and a nearby drinking fountain (used to cook drugs) turned off. These situational facets of the operation reduced the "attractiveness" of the area for drug activity. Sampson and Scott (1999:30) summarize the attractiveness of the site succinctly:

> Running water is a necessity for addicts who shoot up, and its presence was a plus to those driven to use their purchases right away. The abandoned cars also allowed addicts to use drugs without delay. Dealer visibility helped to maintain a customer base; customers did not have to sneak into dark and dangerous alleys to buy drugs. The corner location allowed dealers to see oncoming police, and gave buyers a good view of the market. The couch provided comfort during down times, and the vacant lot offered a secure and unreachable escape route and hideaway.

These examples can be related to the Wilmington study. In Figure 7-3, we reported official data showing that a number of arrests had taken place in the immediate vicinity of Beatty's Safari Lounge. Only when the site was visited and "ground-truthed" to check the local environment did it become clear why the area near this site might have been a haven for drug dealers during the study years.

Across the street from the tavern was a boarded-up and apparently unoccupied building and an over-vegetated patch of waste ground. From a "bars and blocks" perspective, it would have been easy to blame the tavern for the drug market that existed within 400 feet of it. In contrast, from a problem-oriented policing perspective – which included examination of the entire neighborhood surrounding the illegal drug market – it was determined that the tavern was not the focus of the problem. The problem-oriented policing examples we have just discussed from Sampson and Scott (1999) suggest that undesirable urban features, such as poor street lighting, rather than the tavern itself, could have provided incentives for a local drug market.

Similarly, a number of arrests had taken place outside Milton's Liquors during the study period. But the liquor store appears to have been a well-kept establishment. However, across the street from this location was an area that was secluded, poorly lit and overgrown with vegetation. The latter provided an ideal location for drug users who wished to use their goods immediately after purchasing a bottle of alcohol for poly drug use.

By thinking in a problem-oriented policing fashion, and by defining an open-air drug market location as a problem, police can focus on the situational factors that make a location attractive (in other words, viable). Situational crime prevention techniques can then be applied. These techniques have grown over the last few years into a range of 25 techniques, organized into five categories (Cornish and Clarke, 2003) that involve:

- Increasing the effort.

- Increasing the risks.

- Reducing the rewards.

- Reducing provocations.

- Removing excuses.

Many of the 25 techniques can have value in reducing the attraction of a drug market. For example, by *controlling access to facilities* (increasing the effort) the police in Portland were able to remove a haven from drug dealers when they had a building leveled. By adding a reinforced lighting system, the police in Delray Beach were able to *assist natural surveillance* (increasing the risks), and by posting "no trespassing" signs they were able to *post instructions* (removing excuses). In these cases, the spatial context provided the opportunity to run a street drug market. This context included both the opportunities provided by the physical parameters of the landscape as well as the reluctance of the local community to confront the illicit trade (which is a feature of the socio-demographics of the area). Both of these contextual features can be mapped and better understood with the aid of a GIS, and both of these will need to be ground-truthed through visual inspection to get the best picture of the local environment that will have to be changed. The police will not have to conduct high-level statistical analysis such as ZIP models to get their answers. These analyses are left to academics whose most important finding often is not what causes crime, but what does not cause crime (even when conventional wisdom tells us that it does). Such a factor is spatial displacement (Curtis and Sviridoff, 1994; MacNamara, 1994), which is discussed below.

DISPLACEMENT: FRIEND OR FOE?

Finally, it is worth considering the prospect of displacement. Displacement is the likelihood that if police intervene in some way at location A, then the drug problem will simply move to place B (MacNamara, 1994). The perception that some crime interventions can demonstrate total displacement – the complete movement of an amount of crime from one place to another – is common but has little evidential basis. As Eck (1998:5) notes, " . . . concern about displacement is usually based more on pessimism than empirical fact." Testing for displacement is a worthwhile venture, as is testing for a diffusion of benefits stemming from the benefits of a police intervention extending beyond the limits of the individual operational area. For example, if agglomeration economies exist at a site because it has become widely known as a place to purchase drugs, police activities at this site can change the perception so that this becomes not a good place to purchase drugs. Newspaper stories on public agency response to a drug market can help in this regard (Graham and Ott, 2004).

Significant concerns about displacement appear to be relatively unfounded, yet are commonly voiced by the public, the media and criminal justice professionals (MacNamara, 1994). These fears should certainly not be heeded as a reason to resist a crime prevention initiative. In a recent review of the literature, there appears to be as much evidence for a diffusion of crime prevention benefits as for any spatial displacement (Ratcliffe, 2002).

Given the economic viability that individual locations can have for the drug business, even if displacement were detected it may be of overall gain to the police and the community. The dealers are reluctant to change their locations. There are sound financial reasons for this, as many cops intuitively know (Weisburd and Mazerolle, 2000:18):

> According to the detectives, dealers tend to sell the same drug in the same area, providing a kind of specialization of market activities. These dealers do not drift considerably from one day to the next because, if they do, customers will not know where to find the drug of their choice. Although we were initially skeptical of this assumption of specialization at discrete places, our own analysis of the type of drug confiscated during arrests generally confirmed the detectives' conclusion.

Is Displacement a Positive Outcome?

We argue here that displacement may be a positive outcome from a policing perspective. Given that total displacement is rare, displacement of a street drug market will move dealers to locations that are less ideal than the location that they initially chose and were displaced from. Consider that if the second location was better from an economic perspective, why were they not there in the first place? If they are moved to a less attractive site, then the financial rewards of the lesser site will not be as high as the first location. If the financial rewards are not as high, this implies that fewer drugs are sold, especially to the young and to dabblers (Kleiman, 1988; Knutsson, 2000). It may be that the police have not been able to curtail the drug market completely, but they have nevertheless significantly constrained drug activity and forced dealers to a less rewarding area. If the next police problem-oriented operation is targeted to the second site, and the dealers are moved to an even less attractive location, then the drug market is now sited at the third best location in the area. Eventually, the available market will not be sufficient to sustain the drug trade at this (or subsequent) locations, reducing the crime problem for local police and local communities.

FINAL THOUGHTS

The goal of this book is to encourage the police and public to think geographically and economically. We hope they think beyond punitive tactics such as source-country interdiction and arrests in local areas to a problem-oriented approach to drugs in our society. We are in complete agreement with Kleiman and Young (1995:746) when they state:

> . . . focusing on a criminal organization or individual as the unit of analysis may be less helpful than focusing on a geographic area. By determining which factors are scarce and can most easily be targeted in a particular locale, those working to combat the drug problem can increase the use of a range of tactics rather than focus primarily on those that involve arrest.

This approach means working in cooperation with other agencies of government. As noted by Stewart (1988:v): "No single agency can fulfill, through its own efforts, the public's justifiable demand that we rid our communities of drug abuse and the crime and violence it fosters . . . interagency cooperation at all levels of government is an essential ingredient of successful drug strategies."

One important finding of the analyses in this book is that policy should not focus outward when addressing illegal drugs at the higher levels of distribution and should not focus inward when addressing illegal drugs at the local levels of distribution. Both are a form of "blaming" that distracts us from the true problem. On the international scale, we should not blame producing countries (for reasons outlined in the first chapter). At the local level, we should not blame features of the built environment such as taverns or homeless shelters. In the analysis reported above, it was determined that illegal drug-sales arrests cluster spatially around many of these features. The theoretical reason given is that these facilities bring together at one site many potential customers for illegal drugs. However, not all of these facilities that bring together potential customers attracted illegal drug dealers. In fact, it is not so much the facility as its setting within the city and the surrounding land use that is important. We need to determine the surrounding land use or misuse, such as neighboring abandoned property, parks and playgrounds that in combination create environments conducive to illegal drug dealing.

We also must consider the size of the areas over which place managers can be expected to exercise control (Eck, 1998). Clearly, tavern owners and managers are expected to control the activities that take place within their establishments. However, they are not, as yet, expected to control activities on the street on the entire city block of their establishments. Ideally, one should identify drug arrests that take place within an establishment before assigning blame. Drug sales that take place outside may be due as much to the unmeasured surrounding environment as to the establishment itself. Often, these are factors that can be observed by public officials.

The police officers who patrol on a daily basis are in a unique position to determine what the problems of a particular site are. In tackling these problems, the police should be encouraged to think beyond their traditional role as crime fighters into a new role as problem solvers. This may be a difficult task. Just as it is easier to "spank" a child than to identify and correct what really led to the misbehavior, it is easier to arrest drug dealers than to determine why they are dealing from a specific location and correct the problem. Our goal is to move public officials beyond "spanking" toward problem solving, and to move away from "spraying roaches" again and again to discovering the social and economic environmental conditions that attract the roaches in the first place.

NOTES

1. Under common law principles, courts have the authority to order the abatement of public nuisances, and drug-dealing premises have been held to qualify (Caldwalander et al., 1993; Kleiman and Young, 1995).

2. "Bawdy-house" laws were designed to close houses of prostitution. In some states, these laws specifically allow the closure of premises used for illicit trade, such as the sale of illegal drugs (Kleiman and Young, 1995).

3. Premises can be summarily closed in some states for violations of fire, health, safety, and building codes. In Tampa, the assignment of a city code-enforcement officer to the QUAD program resulted in the closing of many drug-infested locations (Kennedy, 1993).

4. Federal Racketeering-Influenced and Corrupt Organizations (RICO) laws allow for the confiscation and forfeiture of property

used for illegal purposes, such as selling illegal drugs. The threat of forfeiture can be used to encourage landlords to evict drug dealers from their properties.

5. Parking and traffic enforcement refers to the fact that drug buyers often double-park or stop in traffic lanes to bargain for illegal drugs. Stricter enforcement of traffic laws in drug-dealing locations makes it more difficult for buyers to purchase drugs.

6. Checkpoints are sometimes set up by the local police to keep nonresidents out of drug-dealing neighborhoods. This tactic is somewhat similar to the gated communities occupied by the wealthy in exclusive suburbs, where you must prove you are a resident to enter the community.

7. Anti-drug citizens' groups can make it unpleasant to purchase drugs by drawing attention to the fact that a drug deal is taking place. This is done by creating noise and using picket signs to advertise who is buying drugs in their neighborhoods. In Washington Square in New York City, such a citizens' group of women referred to themselves as the "Pots and Pans." They would bang on pots and pot lids to draw attention to drug transactions (Rengert, 1996).

8. Target hardening refers to the use of improved locks, bars, and/ or alarms on property to make it more difficult to break into. It is designed to deter burglary of homes and other property.

9. Anti-prostitution efforts refer to the fact that many illegal drug users fund their drug habits by engaging in prostitution. By more strictly enforcing prostitution laws, police make it more difficult for some users to obtain funds to finance their illegal drug habits.

10. Restitution orders for drug-involved offenders require that victims of crime be repaid for their losses. This makes it less likely that the proceeds of crime can be used for purchasing illegal drugs.

11. "Sell and bust operations" involved police officers disguised as dealers selling illegal drugs. Once a buyer makes a purchase, he/ she is subject to arrest.

12. "Turkey dope" refers to undercover police selling inert substances packaged as illegal drugs. This practice discourages users, who find they have wasted good money on bad drugs.

13. Observation arrests are made by police officers who observe a drug transaction. Stopping suspected drug-market participants for questioning can also serve as a deterrent.

14. Car checks and postcards serve as a deterrent when persons who are not neighborhood residents are seen driving through drug-dealing locations. The police can observe and log the license numbers of such cars. Police can then follow up with a postcard to the car owner stating where the vehicle was seen and indicating that the site is known for drug dealing. If the drivers of the cars are the children of the registered vehicle owners, the repercussions of such postcards can be substantial (Kleiman and Young, 1995).

15. "Publicity" is the tactic of publishing in local newspapers the names of persons arrested for purchasing illegal drugs. This publicity is especially troublesome for persons who otherwise lead respectable lives. Fear of being "outed" in the newspaper will deter many people from using illegal drugs.

16. Drug dealers and buyers do not like to have their transactions in plain view. At night, one method of making drug transactions more obvious is to increase or improve the street lighting where drug transactions take place.

17. Checking the ownership records of jewelry and cars can provide police with information on whether a dealer is spending more than he/she is making legitimately. If so, the items purchased with profits from illegal drug sales are subject to forfeiture.

18. Forfeitures refer to the Racketeering-Influenced and Corrupt Organizations (RICO) Act, which is a federal law that authorizes the forfeiture of any goods or property that is used in an illegal enterprise or obtained with funds resulting from criminal activity such as selling illegal drugs.

19. Lookouts for illegal drug dealers are not likely to be sanctioned since they are not directly involved in the illegal transaction. If all participants in an illegal transaction were legally sanctioned, the cost to the entire operation would increase substantially.

20. Field interrogation by the police takes time, and therefore money, from illegal drug dealers. It also signals to buyers that this site is under surveillance, making it a riskier site to do business. Field interrogations announce the presence of the police, which makes a drug dealing location less profitable.

21. In "buy and bust" operations, police disguise themselves as illegal drug users and attempt to purchase drugs from a dealer. If a sale is consummated, the dealer is arrested either by the undercover police officer or by the backup officers.

22. Beat cops can patrol drug-dealing locations under directed patrol, in addition to their random patrol assignment. This additional attention to a drug-dealing location disrupts normal operations and makes the location less profitable than it would be if operations were not disrupted from time to time.

TECHNICAL APPENDIX.
THE MODELING APPROACH USED
IN THIS STUDY

In order to understand the modeling approach used in this research, it is useful to have a clear understanding of the different geographical scales of interaction. On the one hand, there is the existing geography of the census. Census block groups are well recognized, and regressions using census geography are computationally simpler and easier to comprehend and communicate. There is the complication of using the built environment data in the census geography, though that is solvable (see below). The more intractable problem arises from the fact that since the census geography is composed of inflexible and rather arbitrary boundaries, a census unit is likely to be both more inclusive (by incorporating too much heterogeneity) and less specific (because a drug sales arrest allocated to a block group can be located anywhere within that block group) than the reality we are trying to model. The alternative is to create new geographies based not on inflexible and over-encompassing census boundaries, but on the geography created by the built environment itself. The following hypothetical example may clarify this issue.

Consider an area composed of two census block groups (numbered 1 and 2 in Figure A-1). The attributes of the block groups are known from the census, and are presumed to be evenly spread throughout the block groups. Traditional modeling exercises have used these attributes of the block groups to analyze the variance in some phenomenon. However, at least some of the attributes of the block groups are not uniformly distributed within them. For example, the census may indicate that 50% of the housing units in a block group are renter-occupied units. This does not mean that every other unit is a single-family residence. Rather, the rental units are likely to be clustered in one or two complexes (perhaps on one side of the block group) with the remainder

Figure A-1. Schematic for Space-Centered Model

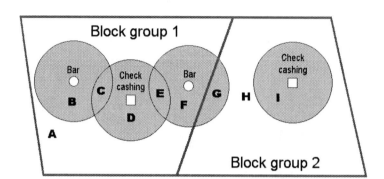

of the housing units being single-family homes. However, the census implies that a single characteristic (such as 50% rental units) is uniformly distributed across a block group or census tract.

A block group can be further subdivided on the basis both of the location of the built environment that is embedded within it, and by the spatial extent of illegal drug sales arrests that theoretically can be linked to such environmental artifacts. Earlier the point was made that all else being equal, the most deleterious influence of a bar or tavern extends to one city block (say 400 feet) surrounding it. A Location Quotient was computed for each buffer to check whether this influence exists.

In the schematic figure shown here (in Figure A-1), the two block groups become subdivided into nine parcels (A through I, based on the locations of the four artifacts shown). Two of these nine parcels (C and E) lie within the zone of inclusion of two artifacts. Hence three types of parcels have been created: (a) without deleterious built environment features (A and H); (b) with one deleterious feature (B, D, F, G, and I); and (c) with two deleterious features (C and E). To put it in another way, when a 400-foot buffer around a liquor store intersects a block group boundary, the block group is divided into two new areas, one that contains the liquor store buffer and one that does not. If the part of the block group that contains the 400-foot liquor store buffer again is intersected by a buffer of 400 feet around a check-cashing store, it is subdivided into new areas that are within 400 feet of a liquor store *and* 400 feet of a check-cashing store, and an area that is within 400 feet of a liquor store but *not* within 400 feet of a check-cashing store. In this manner, using Bayesian logic, quite complex regions are defined.

An alternative approach is to use a vicinity-type modeling strategy, as employed by Ratcliffe and McCullagh in their analysis of burglary victimization in Nottingham, UK (Ratcliffe and McCullagh, 1999). The vicinity approach averages values derived from a number of areal census units in the immediate vicinity of a point feature and then appoints the result as an attribute to the point feature. This form of dasymetric mapping is applicable to the combination of census tract variables, but we have chosen the methodology shown here as it enhances the integration of nearby urban (point) features as well as allowing for an increased number of spatial polygon units, which improves the reliability of the statistical models (described later).

In the Wilmington study area, using the spatial principles outlined in the previous section, over 1,300 parcels or polygons are created and remain available for analysis after we have eliminated the sliver parcels.[1] An example of the complete geography thus created is shown in Figure A-2. The importance of this new geography is that although census variables still must be assumed to be uniformly distributed within census block groups, drug sales arrests are not so constrained. They can be assigned to the new areas associated with built environmental features. In this manner, quite small parcels that are subdivisions of census block groups can be analyzed. In this case, the largest parcels possible would be defined by the size of a census block group. But in most cases, these block groups would be subdivided by the buffers around the built environmental features.

These new geographies or spaces can be understood in three different ways. First, each new parcel may be thought of in binary terms – it has at least one drug sales arrest in it, or it does not have any drug arrests in it. It is then possible to model this distribution to identify those factors that contribute to any drug sale arrest within a parcel – potentially because of low income, or proximity to a tavern, or proximity to a highway exit, and so on. If all three (or four or five) factors have contributed, which of the factors have the strongest influence in determining whether or not a parcel has a drug sales arrest in it? These questions can be answered using a logistic modeling approach.

Logistic models cannot answer questions on the quantity of arrests in a parcel. That is, the logistic models are good for understanding a

Figure A-2. Central Wilmington Space-Centered Polygon Structure

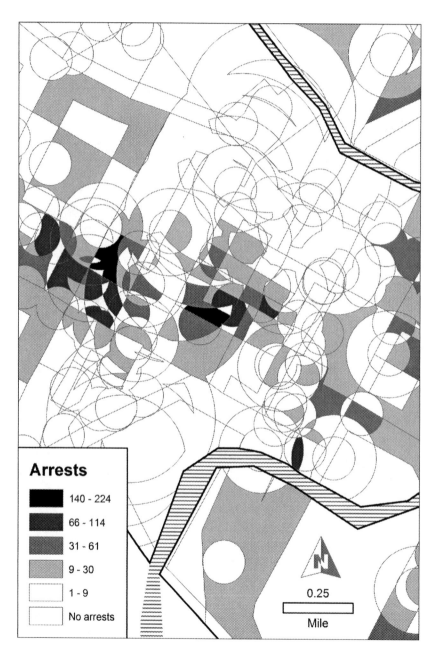

Arrests

■	140 - 224
▨	66 - 114
▨	31 - 61
▨	9 - 30
	1 - 9
	No arrests

0.25

Mile

0-1 distribution, but are unable to provide answers for a distribution that looks similar to this: 0-0-0-0-0-0-1-1-1-2-2-3-9-23-42. This is a special kind of event count distribution, where the majority of units of observation (or parcels in this case) have zero units of the variable being observed (drug sales arrests in this case), a smaller number of parcels have just one arrest each, an even smaller number of parcels have two arrests, and so on until there may be one parcel with 23 arrests and one with 42 arrests. Such distributions are best analyzed using Zero Inflated Poisson (or ZIP) models.

ZERO INFLATED POISSON MODELS

Zero Inflated Poisson (ZIP) models are a form of a dual regime event count model. Dual regime models are those in which the data-generating process may be separated into two distinct phases: the first in which the count moves from zero to some discrete event-count distribution, and the second that generates the observed count. The data take the form of non-negative integers.

An example of a dual regime model is an analysis of the number of children families intend to have. In this case, we assume that a different decision is involved in deciding whether or not to have children (the conflict of dual careers perhaps) versus deciding how many children to have once the couple has decided to have children. The decision of whether or not to have children may be considered as a "hurdle" to be crossed before analysis of how many children the couple decides to have. In the words of Zorn (1998:371):

> The general form of the model analyzes observations that undergo two separate stages in the determination of the final, observed event count. The first transition stage occurs when the observation moves from a state in which the event of interest does not (typically cannot) occur to one in which events occur at some rate . . .

ZIP models are not truncated at zero. They allow for zero counts in the second stage, an important property in the case of an analysis of illicit drug sales arrests. In our theoretical discussion of illegal drug markets, it was proposed that illegal markets would not, and could not, occur at locations that did not reach a threshold level of profitability. But once a threshold level of profitability exists, a varying number of drug dealers (including none) may establish markets at that location. Zorn (1998) points out that the event counts (in our case drug sales arrests) may be over- or under-dispersed. When contagion is present, events are not independent. In the case of positive contagion, the conditional probability of an additional event occurring is positively related to previous events at that location. In other words, the occurrence of one event increases the probability of observing another event at that location. Conversely, if no event occurs, there is less likelihood that an event will occur. Zorn (1998:377) sums up this process thus:

> In this way, high values of the count variable are "pushed" even higher due to the positive dependence of individual events. Conversely, the absence of the occurrence of events in a positively contagious process will result in inertia, so that low values (particularly zeros) on these variables will tend to remain zeros. As a result, positive contagion leads to count data that are over dispersed; the presence of exceptionally high and low counts causes the variance to be large relative to the mean.

This model fits well with the theoretical proposition that once a drug market becomes large, "agglomeration economies" will lead other dealers to establish markets in the same area. In other words, once a threshold condition of profitability has been reached and excess profits begin to accrue at a particular site, competing dealers will establish operations at that site and it will become known as a place to obtain drugs. Therefore, more customers will travel to this location to obtain drugs and ever more competing dealers will establish markets at or near that location. ZIP models are well suited to test the theoretical propositions that form the basis of this analysis.

In the present analysis, Zero Inflated Poisson models are needed since the distribution of event counts has a large number of spaces with zero events. When all years are combined, and the entire city is examined, there are over 1,300 spaces that have been created by the processes of buffering and overlaying. Of these 1,300 plus spaces, 831 of the spaces have zero arrest events within them. This amounts to 63% of the spaces. Of the remaining parcels, the largest number have only one arrest within them, the next largest count is two arrests, and so on until one parcel has over 200 arrests within it.

Clearly, the Wilmington data fit nicely into a Zero Inflated Poisson model for analysis. The interpretation of the model is relatively straightforward. In order to identify the significant contributors, we inspect the level of significance of the individual parameter estimates.

This is the modeling approach used. Each parcel is assigned a value of 1 for each built environment feature that it is proximate to. For instance, a parcel may be within 400 feet of a tavern and within 400 feet of a liquor store; in this case, it will be assigned values of 1 for taverns and 1 for liquor stores, and 0 for the six remaining built environment variables (check-cashing stores, I-95, and so on).

Spatial Autocorrelation and Spatial Lag

A final note on the concept of *spatial autocorrelation* may be useful. Most events are not homogeneously distributed over space; rather they tend to form clusters, being similarly affected by similar processes. This property of spatial clustering is also known as spatial autocorrelation – being positive when like values cluster together, and negative when unlike values cluster (see Cliff and Ord, 1981; Odland, 1988). When spatial autocorrelation is present in a distribution, it creates problems similar to those created by serial autocorrelation in time-series data, and therefore it is necessary to correct for it. For example, it may not be the nature of a built environmental feature that accounts for the number of drug sales in a location, but rather agglomeration economies associated with a neighboring site. The existence of agglomeration economies associated with a neighboring site can cause misleading interpretations of the importance of the built environment located at that site.

This property of clustering can be quantified and mapped in several ways, especially through the use of "spatial lag" values calculated as the sum of values for the dependent variable in surrounding parcels. That is, for a given parcel *i*, its spatial lag is the sum of drug sales arrests in the parcels adjoining the parcel *i*. These spatial lag values will become important corrective terms in the model that will be estimated (as discussed below).

The Model Definition

A geography-based ZIP model is used to estimate the factors that contribute to the existence and to the intensity or variation of drug sales in the parcels created by GIS buffers and their spatial overlaps. The models will take the form:

$$y = a + b_1X_1 + b_2X_2 + b_3X_3 + C + e .... (1)$$

Where, y will take a value equal to the number of drug sales arrests within a parcel.

X_1 represents a set of variables pertaining to susceptibility, variables that are all taken from the 1990 census of population and housing. The susceptibility variables that we analyzed include the following:

(1)   percent of female-headed households with children under five;

(2)   percent of unemployed males;

(3)   median household income;

(4)   percent of vacant homes;

(5)   proportion of residents residing in present homes five years ago;

(6)   percent of renter-occupied units; and,

(7)   percent of non-white residents.

X_2 represents a set of variables on accessibility, which includes:

(1)   exits from Interstate Highway I-95; and,

(2)   major transit nodes.

X_3 represents the second set of built environment factors, or the destinations of routine activities. The variable set includes:

(1)   check-cashing stores;

(2)   liquor stores;

(3)   homeless shelters;

(4)   social service program locations; and,

(5)   taverns.

C represents the corrective or control variables that are:

(1)   the spatial lag term, that is not only a correction for spatial auto-correlation but can be interpreted to quantify the degree of local clustering.; and,

(2)   The area of parcels to correct for the variation in parcel size.

NOTES

1.   Note that some of these newly created parcels may be quite small, so small as to have no significant social meaning. In the analysis to

follow, we have ignored all such very small parcels or slivers that in area were less than 0.01% (or one-hundredth of 1%) of the study area.

REFERENCES

Anderson, E. (1999). *Code of the Street: Decency, Violence, and the Moral Life of the Inner City.* New York: W.W. Norton.
—— (1998). "The Social Ecology of Youth Violence." In: M. Tonry and M. Moore (eds.), *Youth Violence.* (Crime and Justice series, vol. 24.) Chicago, IL: University of Chicago Press.

Ball, J.C. (1991). "The Similarity of Crime Rates Among Male Heroin Addicts in New York City, Philadelphia, and Baltimore." *The Journal of Drug Issues* 21: 413-427.

Barlow, D.E. and M.H. Barlow (1999). "A Political Economy of Community Policing." *Policing: An International Journal of Police Strategies & Management* 22(4):646-674.

Barnett, A. (1988). "Drug Crackdowns and Crime Rates: A Comment on the Kleiman Paper." In: M. Chaiken (ed.), *Street-Level Drug Enforcement: Examining the Issues.* Washington, DC: National Institute of Justice.

Baumer, E. (2002). "Neighborhood Disadvantage and Police Notification by Victims of Violence." *Criminology* 40:579-616.

Bauza, A. (1988). "Evaluating Street-Level Drug Enforcement." In: M. Chaiken (ed.), *Street-Level Drug Enforcement: Examining the Issues.* Washington, DC: National Institute of Justice.

Becker, H. (1953). "Becoming a Marijuana User." *American Journal of Sociology* 59:235-242.

Berry, B. and J. Kasarda (1977). *Contemporary Urban Ecology.* New York: Macmillan.

Bevis, C. and J. Nutter (1977). "Changing Street Layouts to Reduce Residential Burglary." Paper presented to the annual meeting of the American Society of Criminology, Atlanta, November.

Block, R. (1995). "Effects of Rapid Transit Stations on Patterns of Street Robbery In Chicago." Paper presented at the annual meetings on Crime Prevention Through Environmental Design, Cambridge, England.

Block, R and S. Davis (1996). "The Environs of Rapid Transit Stations: A Focus for Street Crime or Just Another Risky Place?" In: R.V. Clarke (ed.), *Preventing Mass Transit Crime.* (Crime Prevention Studies, vol. 8.) Monsey, NY: Criminal Justice Press.

Boba, R. (2003). *Problem Analysis in Policing.* Washington, DC: Police Foundation.

Bohm, R.M., K.M. Reynolds and S.T. Holmes (2000). "Perceptions of Neighborhood Problems and their Solutions: Implications for Community Policing." *Policing: An International Journal of Police Strategies & Management* 23(4):439-465.

Bostrom, D. (2000). Personal communication with the Director of Public Safety for the city of Wilmington, November, 10.

Boyum, D. (1992). "Reflections on Economic Theory and Drug Enforcement." Unpublished Ph.D. thesis in Public Policy, Harvard University, Cambridge, MA.

Brantingham, P. and P. Brantingham (1995a). "Criminality of Place: Crime Generators and Crime Attractors." *European Journal of Criminal Policy and Research* 3(3):5-26.

———— and P. Brantingham (1995b). "Location Quotients and Crime Hotspots in the City." In: C. Block, M. Dabdoub and S. Fregly (eds.), *Crime Analysis through Computer Mapping*. Washington, DC: Police Executive Research Forum.

Breci, M.G. (1997). "The Transition to Community Policing: The Department's Role in Upgrading Officers' Skills." *Policing: An International Journal of Police Strategies & Management* 20(4):766-776.

Bursik, R. (1988). "Social Disorganization and Theories of Crime and Delinquency: Problems and Prospects." *Criminology* 26:519-552.

Caulkins, J. (1998). "What Price Data Tell Us About Drug Markets." *Journal of Drug Issues* 28(3):593-612.

———— and P. Reuter (1998). "What Can We Learn From Drug Prices?" *Journal of Drug Issues* 28:593-612.

Carter, D.L. (1995). *Community Policing and D.A.R.E.: A Practitioner's Perspective.* (BJA Bulletin No. NCJ 154275.) Washington, DC: Bureau of Justice Assistance.

Center for Problem-oriented Policing (2004). (http://www.cops.usdoj.gov/default.asp?Item=36; accessed 24 June 2004.)

Chainey, S. and J.H. Ratcliffe (2005). *GIS and Crime Mapping*. London: Wiley.

Chawla, S. (2004). "How to Develop More Effective Policies Against Crime: Some Reflections on Drugs and Crime Research in an International Context." *European Journal on Criminal Policy and Research* 10(1):85-98.

Clayton, R.R., A.M. Cattarello and B.M. Johnstone (1996). "The Effectiveness of Drug Abuse Resistance Education (Project DARE): Five-year Follow-up Results." *Preventive Medicine* 25:307-318.

Cliff, A. and J. Ord (1981). *Spatial Processes: Models and Applications.* London, UK: Pion.

Cohen, L. and M. Felson (1979). "Social Change and Crime Rate Trends: A Routine Activity Approach." *American Sociological Review* 44:588-608.

COPS (Office of Community Oriented Policing Services) (2004). (www.cops.usdoj.gov; accessed 16 June 2004.)

Cordner, G.W. (1995). "Community Policing: Elements and Effects." *Police Forum* 5(3):1-8.

Cornish, D.B. and R.V. Clarke (2003). "Opportunities, Precipitators and Criminal Decisions: A Reply to Wortley's Critique of Situational Crime Prevention." In: M. Smith and D.B. Cornish (eds.), *Theory for Practice in Situational Crime Prevention.* (Crime Prevention Studies, vol. 16.) Monsey, NY: Criminal Justice Press.

Correia, M.E. (2000). "The Conceptual Ambiguity of Community in Community Policing: Filtering The Muddy Waters." *Policing: An International Journal of Police Strategies & Management* 23(2):218-232.

Cose, E. (1994). "Drawing Up Safer Cities." *Newsweek* 124(2) July:57.

CPC (Community Policing Consortium) (1994). *Understanding Community Policing: A Framework for Action.* Washington DC. (http://www.communitypolicing.org/framework.htm)

Curtis, R. and T. Wendel (1998). "Towards the Development of a Typology of Illegal Drug Markets." Paper presented to the Committee on Data and Research for Policy on Illegal Drugs, National Research Council, Division on Social and Economic Studies, Washington, DC, May 19-21.

———— and M. Sviridoff (1994). "The Social Organization of Street Level Drug Markets and Its Impact on the Displacement Effect." In: R. MacNamara (ed.), *Crime Displacement: The Other Side of Prevention.* East Rockaway, NY: Cummings and Hathaway.

DARE (Drug Abuse Resistance Education) (2004). "D.A.R.E. Works . . . and We Can Prove It!" Report of 2001 Illinois DARE assessment by Dr. Joseph Donnermeyer of Ohio State University. (http://www.dare.com/home/tertiary/Default3ade.asp?N=Tertiary&S=5; accessed June 24, 2004.)

Davies, R.L. (1984). *Store Location and Store Assessment Research.* New York: John Wiley.

Davis, R.C., A.J. Lurigio and D. Rosenbaum (eds.), (1993). *Drugs and the Community: Involving Community Residents in Combating the Sale of Illegal Drugs.* Springfield, IL: Charles Thomas Publisher.

Drug Availability Steering Committee (2002). *Drug Availability Estimates in the United States.* Washington, DC: Drug Enforcement Administration.

Dunlap, E. (1995). "Inner City Crisis and Drug Dealing: Portrait of a Drug Dealer and His Household." In: S. MacGregor and A. Lipow (eds.), *The Other City: People and Politics in New York and London.* Totowa, NJ: Humanities Press.

———— (1992). "Impact of Drugs on Family Life and Kin Networks in Inner-City African-American Single Parent Households." In: A. Harrell and G. Peterson (eds.), *Drugs, Crime, and Social Isolation: Barriers to Urban Opportunity.* Washington, DC: Urban Institute Press.

Eck, J.E. (2004) "Why Don't Problems Get Solved?" In: W.G. Skogan (ed.), *Community Policing: Can It Work?* Belmont, CA: Wadsworth Thomson.

———— (1998) "Preventing Crime at Places." In: L.W. Sherman, D. Gottfredson, D. MacKenzie, J. Eck, P. Reuter, and S. Bushway (eds.), *Preventing Crime: What Works, What Doesn't, What's Promising.* Washington, DC: National Institute of Justice.

———— (1997). "What Do Those Dots Mean: Mapping Theories with Data." In: D. Weisburd and T. McEwen (eds.), *Crime Mapping and Crime Prevention.* (Crime Prevention Studies, vol. 6.) Monsey, NY: Criminal Justice Press.

———— (1994). "Drug Markets and Drug Places: A Case-Control Study of the Spatial Structure of Illegal Drug Dealing." Dissertation submitted to the Graduate School of the University of Maryland, College Park, Maryland.

Engstad, P. (1975). "Environmental Opportunities and the Ecology of Crime." In: R. Silverman and J. Teevan (eds.), *Crime in Canadian Society.* Toronto, CAN: Butterworth.

Fagan, J. (1993). "The Political Economy of Drug Dealing Among Urban Gangs." In: R.C. Davis, A.J. Lurigio and D.P. Rosenbaum (eds.), *Drugs and the Community.* Springfield, IL: Charles Thomas Publisher.

Florida (1999). "Health Costs of Illegal Drugs." Tallahassee, FL: Agency for Health Care Administration.

Forsyth, A., R. Hammersley, T. Lavelle and K. Murray (1992). "Geographical Aspects of Scoring Illegal Drugs." *British Journal of Criminology* 32:292-309.

Gelberg, L., L. Linn and B. Leake (1988). "Mental Health, Alcohol and Drug Use, and Criminal History Among Homeless Adults." *American Journal of Psychiatry.* 145:191-196.

Ghosh, A. and S.L. McLafferty (1987). *Location Strategies for Retail and Service Firms.* Lexington, MA: Lexington Books.

Ginsberg, T. (2002). "Breaking the White Horse." *Inquirer Magazine,* December 8:10-17.

Goldstein, H. (1979). "Improving Policing: A Problem-Oriented Approach." *Crime & Delinquency* 25:236-258.

Goode, E. (2005). *Drugs in American Society* (6th ed.). Boston, MA: McGraw Hill.

Goodman, H. (1990). "Herman Wrice: Facing Down the Dealers." *The Philadelphia Inquirer Magazine,* April 1:16-20.

Gottfredson, M. and M. Hindelang (1979). "A Study of the Behavior of the Law." *American Sociological Review* 44:3-18.

Graham, T. and D. Ott (2004). "Camden to Raze the Alley, A Symbol of Troubled Past." *The Philadelphia Inquirer,* July 20, Section B:1.

Hope, T. (1985). "Preventing Alcohol-related Disorder in the City Center: A Case Study." Paper presented at the annual meeting of the American Society of Criminology, San Diego, November.

Hough, M. and M. Edmunds (1997). "Tackling Drug Markets: An Eclectic Approach." Paper read to The 6 International Seminar on Environmental Criminology and Crime Analysis, Oslo, Norway, June.

Inciardi, J.A. (1995). "Heroin Use and Street Crime." In: J.A. Inciardi and K. McElrath (eds.), *The American Drug Scene: An Anthology.* Los Angeles, CA: Roxbury Publishing Company.

——— and A.E. Pottieger (1995). "Kids, Crack, and Crime." In: J.A. Inciardi and K. McElrath (eds.), *The American Drug Scene: An Anthology.* Los Angeles, CA: Roxbury Publishing Company.

——— and D. McBride (1989). "Legalization: A High Risk Alternative in the War on Drugs." *American Behavioral Scientist* 32(3):259-289.

Johnson, B., A. Golub and E. Dunlap (2000). "The Rise and Decline of Drugs, Drug Markets, and Violence in New York City." In: A. Blumstein and J. Wallman (eds.), *The Crime Drop in America.* New York: Cambridge University Press.

Kaplan, J. (1983). *The Hardest Drug: Heroin and Public Policy.* Chicago, IL: University of Chicago Press.

Kennedy, D. (1993). *Closing the Market: Controlling the Drug Trade in Tampa, Florida.* Washington, DC: U.S. Department of Justice, National Institute of Justice.

——— (1990). "Fighting the Drug Trade in Link Valley." (Case number C16-90-935.0, Case Program, John F. Kennedy School of Government.) Cambridge, MA: Harvard University.

Kleiman, M. (1991). "Modeling Drug Markets." Paper presented to the annual meeting of the American Society of Criminology, San Francisco, CA, November.

———— (1988). "Crackdowns: The Effects of Intensive Enforcement on Retail Heroin Dealing." In: M. Chaiken (ed.), *Street Level Enforcement: Examining the Issues*. Washington, DC: National Institute of Justice.

———— and R. Young (1995). "The Factors of Production in Retail Drug-Dealing." *Urban Affairs Review* 30(5):730-748.

Knutsson, J. (2000). "Swedish Drug Markets and Drugs Policy." In: M. Natarajan and M. Hough (eds.), *Illegal Drug Markets: From Research to Prevention Policy*. (Crime Prevention Studies, vol. 11.) Monsey, NY: Criminal Justice Press.

Kornhauser, R. (1978). *Social Sources of Delinquency*. Chicago, IL: University of Chicago Press.

Kraska, P.B. (1990). "The Unmentionable Alternative: The Need For, and The Argument Against, The Decriminalization of Drug Laws." In: R. Weisheit (ed.), *Drugs, Crime and the Criminal Justice System*. Cincinnati, OH: Anderson Publishing.

Lacayo, R. (1989). "On the Front Lines." *Time*, September 11:14-18.

Laub, J. (1980). "Ecological Considerations in Victim Reporting to the Police." *Journal of Criminal Justice* 9:419-430.

Lersch, K. (2004). *Space, Time, and Crime*. Durham, NC: Carolina Academic Press.

Leslie, A. (1971). "A Benefit-Cost Analysis of New York City's Heroin Addiction Problems and Programs-1971." New York: Health Services Administration.

Levine, N. and M. Wachs (1986). "Bus Crime in Los Angeles: I – Measuring the Incidence." *Transport Research* 20(4):273-284.

———— M. Wachs and E. Shirazi (1986). "Crime at Bus Stops: A Study of Environmental Factors." *Architectural and Planning Research* 3:339-361.

Loukaitou-Sideris, A. (1999). "Hot Spots of Bus Stop Crime." *Journal of the American Planning Association* 65(4):395-411.

———— R. Liggett and H. Iseki (2002). "The Geography of Transit Crime." *Journal of Planning Education and Research* 22:135-151.

MacNamara, R. (1994). *Crime Displacement: The Other Side of Prevention*. East Rockaway, NY: Cummings and Hathaway.

Maier, P. (1989). "The Effects of Taverns and Lounges on Homicides in Residential Areas." Unpublished master's thesis, Kansas State University, Manhattan.

Maltz, M. (1993). "Crime Mapping and the Drug Market Analysis Program (DMAP)." In: C.R. Block and M. Dabdoub (eds.), *Workshop of Crime Analysis Through Computer Mapping, Proceedings: 1993*. Chicago, IL: Illinois Criminal Justice Information Authority.

Mehay, S. (1973). "The Use and Control of Heroin: An Economic Perspective." *Federal Reserve Bank of Philadelphia: Business Review* (December):14-21.

Metraux, S. and D. Culhane (2004). "Homeless Shelter Use and Reincarceration Following Prison Release." *Criminology and Public Policy* (3):139-160.

Mieczkowski, T. (ed.), (1992). *Drugs, Crime, and Social Policy*. Boston, MA: Allyn and Bacon.

Moore, M. and M. Kleiman (1989). "The Police and Drugs." *Prospectives on Policing. No. 11*. Washington, DC: National Institute of Justice, Office of Justice Programs.

McCoy, H., C. Miles and J. Inciardi (1995). "Survival Sex: Inner-City Women and Crack-Cocaine." In: J. Inciardi and K. McElrath (eds.), *The American Drug Scene: An Anthology*. Los Angeles, CA: Roxbury Publishing Company.

Morenoff, J., R. Sampson and S. Raudenbush (2001). "Neighborhood Inequality, Collective Efficacy, and the Spatial Dynamics of Urban Violence." *Criminology* 39:517-560.

Morganthau, T. (1989). "Children of the Underclass." *Newsweek*, Sept. 11:16-24.

Nadelmann, E. (1992). "Thinking Seriously About Alternatives to Drug Prohibition." *Daedalus* 121(3):85-132.

―――― (1988). "The Case for Legalization." *Public Interest* 92:3-31.

Newman, O. (1973). *Defensible Space.* New York: Collier Books.

Nicholl, J. (2004). "Task Definition." In: J. Ratcliffe (ed.), *Strategic Thinking in Criminal Intelligence.* Sydney, AUS: Federation Press.

Nisbett, R. and D. Cohen (1996). *Culture of Honor: The Psychology of Violence in the South.* Boulder, CO: Westview Press.

Norris, R., K. Harries and J. Nitek (1982). *Geography: An Introductory Perspective.* Toronto, CAN: Charles Merrill Publishing Company.

Odland, J. (1988). *Spatial Autocorrelation.* Newbury Park, CA: Sage Publications.

Office of National Drug Control Policy (2003). *National Drug Control Strategy Update.* Washington, DC, February.

―――― (1997). *Andean Program Review.* (Prepared by the Office of Program, Budget, Research, and Evaluation.) Washington, DC: U.S. Government Printing Office.

Olligschlaeger, A. (1997). "Spatial Analysis of Crime Using GIS-Based Data: Weighted Spatial Adaptive Filtering and Chaotic Cellular Forecasting with Applications to Street Level Drug Markets." Dissertation submitted to the H. John Heinz III School of Public Policy and Management, Carnegie Mellon University, Pittsburgh, PA.

Openshaw, S., A. Cross, M. Charlton, C. Brunsdon and J. Lillie (1990). "Lessons Learnt From a Post Mortem of a Failed GIS." *2nd National Conference and Exhibition of the AGI,* Brighton, UK, pp.2.3.1 – 2.3.5.

Pattillo-McCoy, M. (1999). *Black Picket Fences: Privilege and Peril Among the Black Middle Class.* Chicago, IL: University of Chicago Press.

Pease, K. (2001). "What To Do About It? Let's Turn Off Our Minds and GIS." In: A. Hirschfield and K. Bowers (eds.), *Mapping and Analysing Crime Data.* London, UK: Taylor & Francis.

Pettiway, L. (1995). "Copping Crack: The Travel Behavior of Crack Users." *Justice Quarterly* 12:499-524.

―――― (1994). "Travel Behavior of Crack Users: Implications for Law Enforcement and Drug Control." University of Delaware, Division of Criminal Justice. Unpublished manuscript.

―――― (1993). "The Drug and Criminal Activities Patterns of Urban Offenders: a Markov Chain Analysis." Paper presented to the annual meeting of the International Association of Time Use Research, University of Amsterdam, Netherlands, June.

Pulse Check (2002). *Trends in Drug Abuse.* Washington, DC: Office of National Drug Control Policy.

Quarmby, N. (2004). "Futures Work in Strategic Criminal Intelligence." In: J. Ratcliffe (ed.), *Strategic Thinking in Criminal Intelligence.* Sydney, AUS: Federation Press.

Rasmussen, D., B. Benson and D. Sollars (1993). "Spatial Competition in Illicit Drug Markets: The Consequences of Increased Drug Law Enforcement." *The Review of Regional Studies* 23:219-236.

Ratcliffe, J. (2005) "The Effectiveness of Police Intelligence Management: A New Zealand Case Study." *Police Practice and Research* 6(5).

—— (2004a). "Crime Mapping Techniques at the Start of the 21st Century and the Potential Contribution to Crime Reduction." *European Journal on Criminal Policy and Research* 10(1):65-83.

—— (2004b). *Strategic Thinking in Criminal Intelligence.* Sydney, AUS: Federation Press.

—— (2002). "Burglary Reduction and the Myth of Displacement." *Trends and Issues in Crime and Criminal Justice,* No. 232. Canberra: Australian Institute of Criminology.

—— and M. McCullagh (1999). "Burglary, Victimisation, and Social Deprivation." *Crime Prevention and Community Safety: An International Journal* 1(2):37-46.

Read, T. and D. Oldfield (1995). "Local Crime Analysis." *Police Research Group: Crime Detection and Prevention Series* Paper 65: 61.

Rengert, G. (1996). *The Geography of Illegal Drugs.* Boulder, CO: Westview Press.

—— (1989). "Drug Sales, Residential Burglary and Neighborhood Viability: Sorting Out the Components of a Diffusion Process." *Proceedings. Middle States Division of the Association of American Geographers.* 83-89.

—— S. Chakravorty, T. Bole and K. Henderson (2000). "A Geographic Analysis of Illegal Drug Markets." In: M. Natarajan and M. Hough (eds.), *Illegal Drug Markets.* (Crime Prevention Studies, vol. 11.) Monsey, NY: Criminal Justice Press.

—— and J. Wasilchick (2000). *Suburban Burglary: A Tale of Two Suburbs.* Springfield, IL: Charles Thomas Publisher.

—— and S. Chakravorty (1995). "Illegal Drug Sales and Drug Free School Zones." Paper presented to the annual meeting of the Association of American Geographers, Chicago, March.

—— and A. Rengert (1989). "Marketing Principles and the Spatial Diffusion of an Illegal Drug." Paper presented to the annual meeting of The Association of American Geographers, Boston, Massachusetts, April.

—— and J. Wasilchick (1985). *Suburban Burglary: A Time and A Place for Everything.* Springfield, IL: Charles Thomas Publisher.

Reuter, P. (2000). "The Measurement of Local Drug Markets." Paper presented to the National Institute of Justice Conference on Drug Markets, Washington DC, February 14.

—— (1997). "Why Can't We Make Prohibition Work Better? Some Consequences of Ignoring the Unattractive." *Proceedings of the American Philosophical Society* 141(3):262-275.

—— (1992). "Hawks Ascendant: The Punitive Trend of American Drug Policy." *Daedalus* 121(3):15-38.

—— (1990). "Can the Borders be Sealed?" In: R. Weisheit (ed.), *Drugs, Crime and the Criminal Justice System.* Cincinnati, OH: Anderson Publishing.

—— and R. MacCoun (1992). "Street Drug Markets in Inner-City Neighborhoods: Matching Policy to Reality." In: J. Steinberg, D. Lyon and M. Vaiana (eds.),

Urban America: Policy Choices for Los Angeles and the Nation. Santa Monica, CA: Rand Corporation.

———— and M. Kleiman (1986). "Risks and Prices: An Economic Analysis of Drug Enforcement." In: M. Tonry and N. Morris (eds.), *Crime and Justice: An Annual Review of Research, vol. 7.* Chicago, IL: University of Chicago Press.

Robinson, J. (2003). "The Drug Free Zones, the Police, Locations, and Trends in Drug Sales in Portland, Oregon, 1990-1998." A dissertation submitted to the Department of Criminal Justice, Temple University.

———— B. Lawton, R. Taylor and D. Perkins (2003). "Multilevel Longitudinal Impacts of Incivilities: Fear of Crime, Expected Safety, and Block Satisfaction." *Journal of Quantitative Criminology* 19:237-274.

Roncek, D. and P. Maier (1991). "Bars, Blocks and Crimes Revisited: Linking the Theory of Routine Activities to the Empiricism of 'Hot Spots.'" *Criminology* 29(4):725-753.

———— and M. Pravatiner (1989). "Additional Evidence that Taverns Enhance Nearby Crime." *Sociology and Social Research* 73:185-188.

———— and D. Faggiani (1985). "High Schools and Crime." *The Sociological Quarterly* 26:491-505.

———— and A. Lobosco (1983). "The Effect of High Schools on Crime in their Neighborhoods." *Social Science Quarterly* 64:598-613.

———— and R. Bell (1981). "Bars, Blocks, and Crimes." *Journal of Environmental Systems* 11:35-47.

Rosenbaum, D. and G. Hanson (1998). "Assessing the Effects of School-based Drug Education: A Six-year Multilevel Analysis of Project D.A.R.E." *Journal of Research in Crime and Delinquency* 35(4):381-412.

———— R. Flewelling, S. Bailey, C. Ringwalt and D. Wilkinson (1994). "Cops in the Classroom: A Longitudinal Evaluation of Drug Abuse Resistance Education (DARE)." *Journal of Research in Crime and Delinquency* 31:3-31.

Rossmo, D.K. (2000). *Geographic Profiling.* Boca Raton, FL: CRC Press.

Rushton, G. (1969). "Analysis of Spatial Behavior by Revealed Space Preferences." *Annals of the Association of American Geographers* 59:391-400.

Sadd, S. and R. Grime (1995a). "Innovative Neighborhood-Oriented Policing: Descriptions of Programs in Eight Cities." (Final report.) Washington, DC: National Institute of Justice.

———— and R. Grime (1995b). "Issues in Community Policing: Lessons Learned in the Implementation of Eight Innovative Neighborhood-oriented Policing Programs." (Final report.) Washington, DC: National Institute of Justice.

Sampson, R., J. Morenoff and F. Earls (1999). "Beyond Social Capital: Spatial Dynamics of Collective Efficacy for Children." *American Sociological Review* 64:633-660.

———— and M. Scott (1999). "Tackling Crime and Other Public-Safety Problems: Case Studies in Problem-Solving." Washington, DC: U.S. Department of Justice, Office of Community Oriented Policing Services.

Schuerman, L. and S. Kobrin (1986). "Community Careers in Crime." In: A. Reiss and M. Tonry (eds.), *Communities and Crime.* (Crime and Justice series, vol. 8.) Chicago, IL: University of Chicago Press.

Scott, M. (2003). *The Benefits and Consequences of Police Crackdowns*. (Problem-Oriented Guides for Police, Response Guides Series #1.) Washington, DC: Office of Community Oriented Policing Services.

Shaw, C. and H. McKay (1942). *Juvenile Delinquency and Urban Areas: A Study of Rates of Delinquents in Relation to Different Characteristics of Local Communities in American Cities*. Chicago, IL: University of Chicago Press.

Sherman, L. (1990). "Police Crackdowns: Initial and Residual Deterrence." In: M. Tonry and N. Morris (eds.), *Crime and Justice: An Annual Review of Research* (vol. 12). Chicago, IL: University of Chicago Press.

—— D. Gottfredson, D. MacKenzie, J. Eck, P. Reuter and S. Bushway (1998). *Preventing Crime: What Works, What Doesn't, What's Promising*. Washington, DC: National Institute of Justice.

—— P. Gartin and M. Buerger (1989). "Hot Spots of Predatory Crime." *Criminology* 27:27-55.

Sigler, R. and G. Talley (1995). "Drug Abuse Resistance Education Program Effectiveness." *American Journal of Police* 14(3/4):111-121.

Skogan, W. (1990). *Disorder and Decline: Crime and the Spiral of Decay in American Neighborhoods*. New York: Free Press.

—— and S. Hartnett (1997). *Community Policing, Chicago Style*. New York: Oxford University Press.

Smith, S. (1986). *Crime, Space and Society*. London, UK: Cambridge University Press.

Smith, W., S. Frazee and E. Davison (2000). "Furthering the Integration of Routine Activity and Social Disorganization Theories: Small Units of Analysis and the Study of Street Robbery as a Diffusion Process." *Criminology* 38:489-521.

Snow, D., S. Baker and L. Anderson (1989). "Criminality and Homeless Men: An Empirical Assessment." *Social Problems* 36:532-549.

Stewart, J. (1988). "Foreword." In: M. Chaiken (ed.), *Street-Level Drug Enforcement: Examining the Issues*. Washington, DC: National Institute of Justice.

Taylor, R. (1995). "The Impact of Crime on Communities." *Annals of the American Academy of Political and Social Science* 539:28-45.

Trebach, A. (1987). *The Great Drug War*. New York: MacMillan.

Tilley, N. (2003). "Community Policing, Problem-oriented Policing and Intelligence-led Policing." In: T. Newburn (ed.), *Handbook of Policing*. Cullompton, Devon, UK: Willan.

Turner, S. (1969). "Delinquency and Distance." In: T. Sellin and M. Wolfgang (eds.), *Delinquency: Selected Studies*. New York: John Wiley.

Uchida, C., B. Forst and S. Annan (1992). *Modern Policing and the Control of Illegal Drugs: Testing New Strategies in Two American Cities*. Washington, DC: National Institute of Justice.

UNDOC (United Nations Office on Drugs and Crime) (2003). *Afghanistan Opium Survey 2003: Executive Summary*. Vienna, October.

U.S. Department of Health and Human Services (1993). *National Household Survey of Drug Abuse: Main Findings 1991*. Rockville, MD: U.S. Department of Health and Human Services, Public Health Service.

Walker, S. and C. Katz (2001). *The Police In America: An Introduction* (4th ed.). Boston, MA: McGraw-Hill.

Weingart, S., F.X. Hartmann and D. Osborne (1994). *Case Studies of Community anti-drug Efforts.* (Research in Brief, NCJ 149316.) Washington, DC: National Institute of Justice.

Weisburd, D. and L. Mazerolle (2000) "Crime and Disorder in Drug Hot Spots: Implications for Theory and Practice in Policing." *Police Quarterly* 3(3):331-349.

———— and L. Green (1995). "Policing Hot Spots: The Jersey City Drug Market Analysis Experiment." *Justice Quarterly* 12:711-735.

Wexler, S. (2003). "The Philadelphia Story." *Law Enforcement Technology* 30 (October):10-16.

Wieczorek, W. and J. Coyle (1996). "Alcohol Outlet Type and Assaults." Paper presented to the Annual meeting of the American Society of Criminology, Chicago, November.

Zedlewski, E. (1989). *Making Confinement Decisions.* Washington, DC: National Institute of Justice.

Zimmer, L. (1987). *Operation Pressure Point: The Disruption of Street-Level Drug Trades in New York's Lower East Side.* New York: Center for Research in Crime and Justice, New York University School of Law.

Zorn, C. (1998). "An Analytic and Empirical Examination of Zero-Inflated and Hurdle Poisson Specifications." *Sociological Methods and Research* 26:368-400.

Zucchino, D. (1993). "Resident Beaten and Shot After Confronting Dealers." *The Philadelphia Inquirer,* May 4, Section A, p. 1.